Magento 1.3 Theme Design

Customize the appearance of your Magento
e-commerce store with Magento's powerful
theming engine

Richard Carter

BIRMINGHAM - MUMBAI

Magento 1.3 Theme Design

First published: July 2009

Production Reference: 2200709

Published by Packt Publishing Ltd.
32 Lincoln Road
Olton
Birmingham, B27 6PA, UK.

ISBN 978-1-847196-64-4

www.packtpub.com

Cover Image by Ed Maclean (edmaclean@gmail.com)

Credits

Author
Richard Carter

Reviewers
Jose Argudo
Kara Heinrichs

Acquisition Editor
David Barnes

Development Editor
Siddharth Mangarole

Technical Editor
Chaitanya Apte

Copy Editor
Leonard D'Silva

Indexer
Rekha Nair

Editorial Team Leader
Abhijeet Deobhakta

Project Team Leader
Lata Basantani

Project Coordinator
Rajashree Hamine

Proofreader
Lesley Harrison

Production Coordinator
Shantanu Zagade

Cover Work
Shantanu Zagade

About the Author

Richard Carter is a web designer situated in the North East of England. Richard worked as a freelance web designer in Leicestershire before attending Durham University, where he met his business partner, Michael Peacock. Not long after meeting, they formed Peacock Carter (`http://www.peacockcarter.co.uk`), a web design agency based in the UK. He currently lives in both York and Durham.

Magento Theme Design is Richard's second book. MediaWiki Skins Design, his second book, focused on creating skins for the popular wiki software behind web sites such as `AboutUs.org` and Wikipedia.

I would like to thank Danni, my partner, and Michael, who have put up with the late nights and the endless head scratching required to complete this book to what become some tight deadlines! Thanks are also due to Packt's publishing team for their help and perseverance in creating this book.

I also have much gratitude for the reviewers, who have undoubtedly improved this book and its focus, and for Varien, for beginning what has become an incredibly powerful ecommerce platform.

Lastly, I'd like to thank you, the reader, for purchasing this book: I hope it is of use to you.

About the Reviewers

Jose Argudo is a web developer from Valencia, Spain. After finishing his studies he started working for a software company, always working with PHP. A language he learned to love. Now, after six years, he is confident in his experience and has started to work as freelance, in an attempt to give his personal vision to the projects he undertakes.

Working with Joomla!, Codeigniter, Cakephp, Jquery, and other known open source technologies and frameworks he expects to build stable and reliable aplications that reflect his desire of making better web experiences.

He has also worked as reviewer in the book *Magento Beginners Guide* and hopes to continue working with Magento related projects.

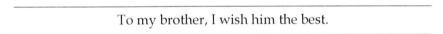

To my brother, I wish him the best.

Kara Heinrichs manages the online operations for the HoMedics companies, which include HoMedics, Salter Housewares, Taylor Precision, Obus Forme, SI Products (brand licensee of The Sharper Image), and Powermat. All of these will be on Magento by the end of the year. Before working for HoMedics, Kara managed the research analysis teams for the government and financial services sectors at ForeSee Results, an online customer satisfaction research company.

She was also Chief Experience Officer and Director of Information Design and Analysis at Fry, an eCommerce design and services company, and taught Web Design and Development at the University of Michigan.

She made her first Magento theme in December 2007 over the Christmas holiday, recreating a site that took another company most of the previous year to implement poorly, and was sold.

Table of Contents

Preface

Magento 1.3 Themes Design takes you through the process of creating themes for Magento Commerce, an open source e-commerce platform. Guiding you through Magento's quirks and vast architecture, Magento 1.3 Themes Design gives you the information you will need to create the ultimate Magento theme.

What this book covers

Chapter 1 introduces Magento, some of its available themes and takes a look at what can be achieved with custom themes.

Chapter 2 provides an overview of how the components of a Magento theme come together to form the final result.

Chapter 3 looks at the basics of Magento theming, from changing your theme's color scheme to changing your logo and setting your theme to display on your store.

Chapter 4 looks at the Magento layout and how to manipulate it to change your store.

Chapter 5 takes a look at non-default themes in Magento, and how you can make use of them to provide a better experience for your customers.

Chapter 6 guides you through Magento themes in greater depth, introducing new methods you can use to improve your store.

Chapter 7 looks at more advanced layout options within Magento, with the goal that readers will become comfortable in creating more advanced layouts for their stores.

Chapter 8 looks at improving your store by integrating social media such as Twitter and other tools to help engage your customers.

Chapter 9 guides you through creating the perfect print style for your Magento store and implementing it for your store.

Chapter 10 takes you through deploying your theme and packaging it as an extension, which you can share with the Magento community.

What you need for this book

You will need an installation of Magento, either on your local machine or on a remote server, your favorite code editor, and permissions to manipulate files.

Who this book is for

This book is for web designers and developers who have experience with CSS and (X)HTML but who are not familiar with the particulars of Magento.

Conventions

In this book, you will find a number of styles of text that distinguish between different kinds of information. Here are some examples of these styles, and an explanation of their meaning.

Code words in text are shown as follows: "We can include other contexts through the use of the `include` directive."

A block of code is set as follows:

```
<title><?php echo $this->getTitle() ?></title>
<meta http-equiv="Content-Type" content="
  <?php echo $this->getContentType() ?>" />
<meta name="description" content="
  <?php echo htmlspecialchars($this->getDescription()) ?>" />
<meta name="keywords" content="
  <?php echo htmlspecialchars($this->getKeywords()) ?>" />
```

When we wish to draw your attention to a particular part of a code block, the relevant lines or items are set in bold:

```
<layout version="0.1.0">
  <default>
    <block type="page/html" name="root" output="toHtml"
      template="page/default.phtml">
    <!—layout continues -->
```

New terms and **important words** are shown in bold. Words that you see on the screen, in menus or dialog boxes for example, appear in the text like this: "clicking the **Next** button moves you to the next screen".

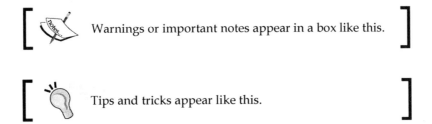

Warnings or important notes appear in a box like this.

Tips and tricks appear like this.

Reader feedback

Feedback from our readers is always welcome. Let us know what you think about this book—what you liked or may have disliked. Reader feedback is important for us to develop titles that you really get the most out of.

To send us general feedback, simply send an email to feedback@packtpub.com, and mention the book title via the subject of your message.

If there is a book that you need and would like to see us publish, please send us a note in the **SUGGEST A TITLE** form on www.packtpub.com or email suggest@packtpub.com.

If there is a topic that you have expertise in and you are interested in either writing or contributing to a book on, see our author guide on www.packtpub.com/authors.

Customer support

Now that you are the proud owner of a Packt book, we have a number of things to help you to get the most from your purchase.

Errata

Although we have taken every care to ensure the accuracy of our content, mistakes do happen. If you find a mistake in one of our books—maybe a mistake in the text or the code—we would be grateful if you would report this to us. By doing so, you can save other readers from frustration, and help us to improve subsequent versions of this book. If you find any errata, please report them by visiting http://www.packtpub. com/support, selecting your book, clicking on the **let us know** link, and entering the details of your errata. Once your errata are verified, your submission will be accepted and the errata added to any list of existing errata. Any existing errata can be viewed by selecting your title from http://www.packtpub.com/support.

Piracy

Piracy of copyright material on the Internet is an ongoing problem across all media. At Packt, we take the protection of our copyright and licenses very seriously. If you come across any illegal copies of our works, in any form, on the Internet, please provide us with the location address or website name immediately so that we can pursue a remedy.

Please contact us at copyright@packtpub.com with a link to the suspected pirated material.

We appreciate your help in protecting our authors, and our ability to bring you valuable content.

Questions

You can contact us at questions@packtpub.com if you are having a problem with any aspect of the book, and we will do our best to address it.

1
Introduction to Magento

Magento Commerce provides a fantastic starting point for an online store. However, for designers with a non-technical background, it is a challenging, but worthwhile opportunity to put your knowledge to the test. In this chapter, we'll look at:

- What Magento is, and what it can do
- The default Magento skin (design)
- Some existing themes from real, "live" stores using Magento

What is Magento?

Magento (http://www.magentocommerce.com) is an open source eCommerce platform, which is renowned for its functionality, but has a reputation of being difficult to theme.

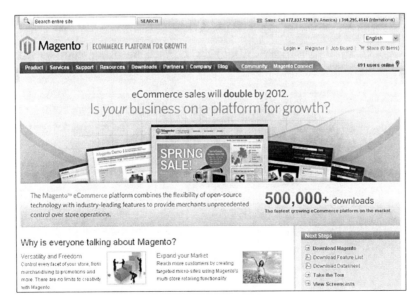

Magento's features

Magento is a feature-rich eCommerce system, which is built on the Zend PHP framework. Magento has all of the features that you would expect of a typical shopping cart and some interesting additions, including:

- Managing multiple stores from one control panel
- Support for localization of languages and currencies
- An **Application Programming Interface (API)**, allowing integration with third-party software
- Search-engine-friendly attributes, such as customizable addresses and auto-generated sitemaps
- RSS feeds for new products
- Tiered pricing, allowing quantity discounts
- Real-time shipping rates from popular couriers
- Integration with many payment gateways including PayPal and `authorize.net`
- Cross-selling
- One-page checkout
- Order and product reporting system
- Automatic image resizing and watermarking

The challenges of theming Magento

Despite its power, Magento has a number of shortcomings, these are:

- Designers can find it more difficult to theme than other open source applications, like WordPress.
- In one way, its modular architecture can be seen as a shortcoming, as this means that making changes to a theme will require multiple files in different directories to be edited (more so than in other software packages).
- The poor-quality or non-existence of documentation.
- The number of technologies that a theme designer needs to be familiar with to theme Magento — XML, PHP, HTML, and CSS.
- The large learning curve for designers who may be familiar with simpler theming systems based upon a small number of templates.

The beauty of an open source eCommerce system such as Magento is that you can help build these features and improve its flaws in to the next release!

It's incredibly rewarding to create a custom theme for your Magento store. As a relatively new and powerful eCommerce system with a growing community to support it, Magento is quickly becoming the next big thing in eCommerce, so learning how to create themes for it is likely to remain important for some time to come.

Default Magento themes

The default Magento theme is called **default**, and provides an attractive, if basic, skeleton design (skin) for your shop.

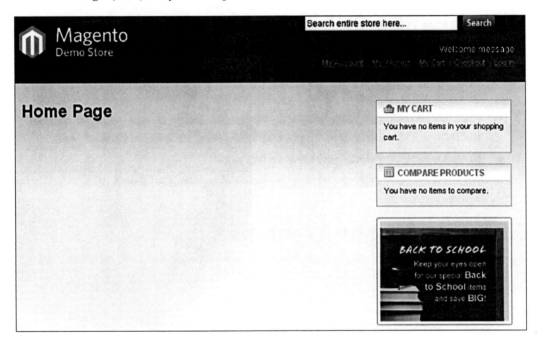

The default skin provides a good framework for the shop, with every element that you want from a shop provided in the location that you would expect. For example, the logo is aligned to the lefthand side by default, and the search feature, account options, and checkout buttons are positioned to the top right of your visitors' screen.

This is common on many web sites, and keeping this consistent in Magento's default theme is wise, as we can assume that your visitors spend more time in total on other web sites than yours. This is where the majority of your store's visitors will look for each of those elements.

The light background color of the main area of the page provides excellent contrast for the content, and the deeper color of the header area, which is described above, helps to establish a visual hierarchy within the page.

It's certainly a clean and smart-looking theme, but as it's the default theme supplied with Magento, it is very generic, and may not be the best choice for your online store, as we'll see.

Why theme your Magento store?

Theming and customizing your Magento store is a great idea if you're aiming to:

- Distinguish your online shop/web site from your competitors
- Increase your sales and enhance your company's profile and its reputation
- Encourage seasonal sales by using Magento's ability to use multiple themes to create a seasonal theme displayed only at the respective time of year
- Remove or alter existing features in Magento
- Adapt to an an existing web site for new or updated business rules

Example Magento themes

Magento allows incredibly customized themes to be created for your store, as these existing Magento stores display.

Raspberry Kids

Raspberry Kids (http://www.raspberrykids.com) is a Magento-powered store selling children's toys. As you can see, the Raspberry Kids' skin is quite different from the default Magento skin, and does a fantastic job of getting across exactly what does the store sell.

Although the Raspberry Kids store retains many of the features of Magento, it is quite different from the default Magento theme. The category page uses a layout similar to many other eCommerce stores, with the customer's cart displayed to the right.

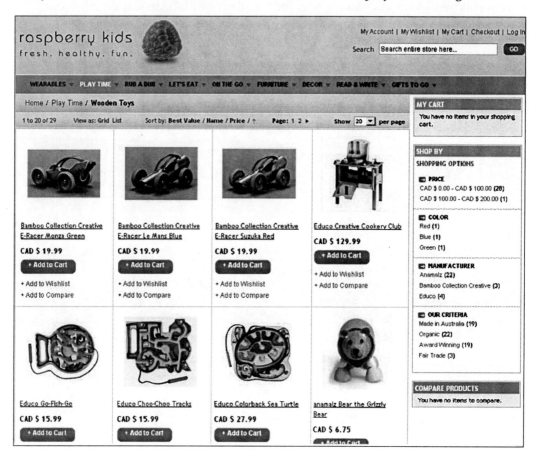

The store also makes the customer's options easy to see in the righthand column, with options to filter products by price, color, and manufacturer.

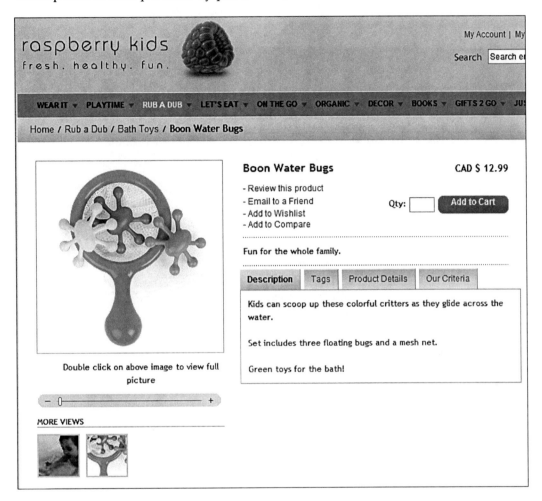

The store's product page has a focus on adding the product to the cart, or interacting with the store, by sending the product to a friend, or reviewing it. The product's details are displayed neatly within tabs so as not to overwhelm the customers with the vast amount of information, which could be displayed about the product.

Mia & Maggie

Mia & Maggie (http://www.miaandmaggie.com) is an online store built using Magento, for selling accessories for pets.

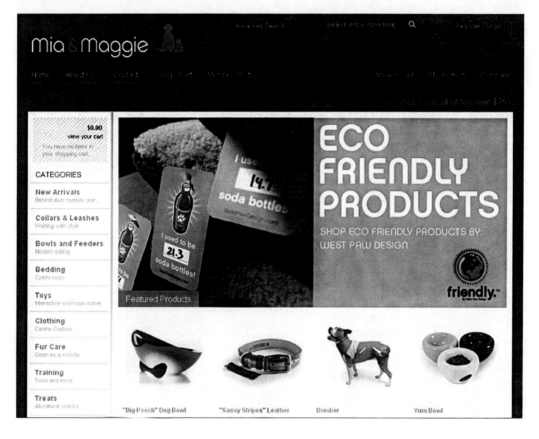

Unusually, the shopping cart is displayed in the left-hand column, which may be a little misleading for some visitors.

The Mia & Maggie store makes good use of Magento's content management system's capabilities, with the main navigation linking to pages about sizing charts for the shoppers' pets, a little information about the company (a touch that aids the reputation of an online store), and a photograph gallery feature. The gallery is a particularly nice touch, as it creates a community around the store, and will undoubtedly help to ensure repeat custom.

The product pages of the store have the picture and name of the products displayed prominently, making use of Magento's wishlist and product comparison features.

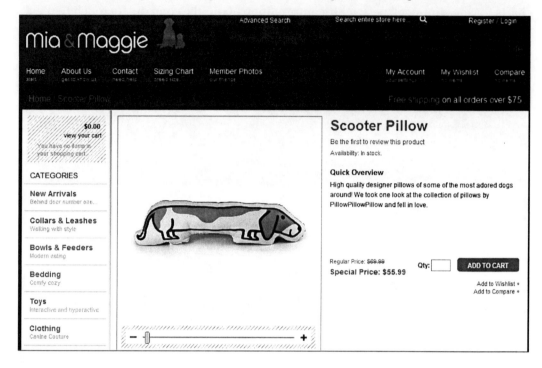

Cacties

Cacties (`http://mycacties.com`) sell designer ties and neckwear on their Magento-powered store.

This store's theme has removed many of the elements from Magento, including the search and shopping cart features, something that may alienate some of the store's visitors.

The category page allows large, high-quality photographs of the products to be displayed, along with the name of the product, while the price and the options to add products to the cart, have been themed out.

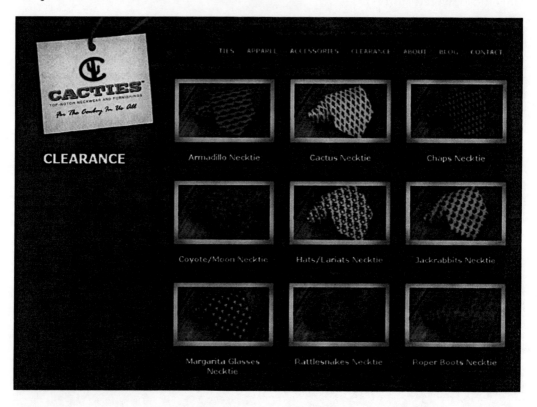

The product view of the Cacties store's Magento theme makes the product's photograph and price the focus of the page.

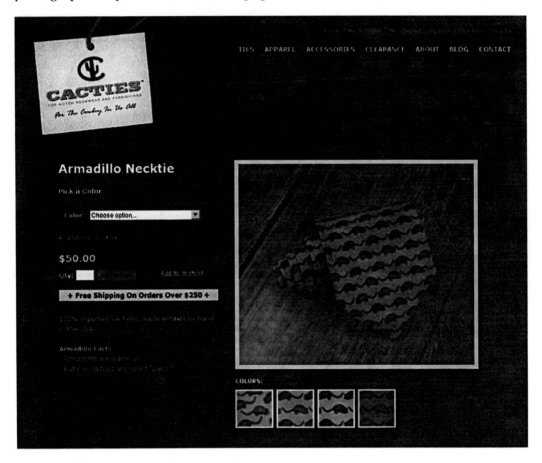

The Recycled Retriever

The Recycled Retriever store (http://www.therecycledretriever.com/store)
sells environment-friendly products for pets.

The Recycled Retriever store is an interesting case to study, as it does not look like a
typical Magento theme. The design is refreshing and clean, clearly mentioning what
does the store sell.

As with the Mia & Maggie store, this store creates a community atmosphere with a
photograph gallery, to which customers are invited to submit their photographs.
The most recent blog post is displayed on the store's homepage too.

In the footer of the skin, there's an option for visitors to sign up for the store's newsletter, allowing more focus to be placed upon products and content.

The category page makes use of more familiar elements, such as the product filtering options and the **ADD TO CART** option, though the wishlist functionality has been removed from the theme.

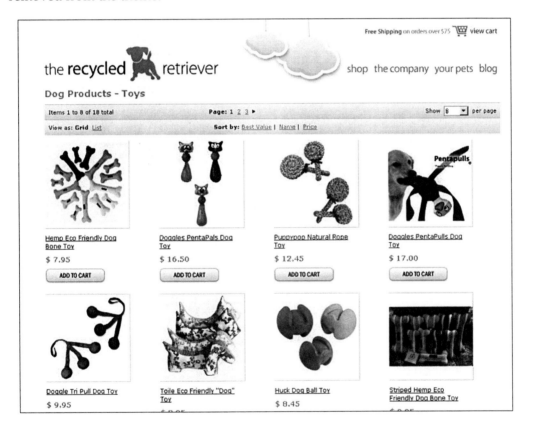

The product page is similarly simple. Options for the product are given focus, along with the product information. The spirit of a community is emphasized again, with the prominent placement of a link to review the product. An overview of the product is given above a more detailed description of the product, and there is the facility to zoom in and out of product photographs, giving the customer a greater idea of what to expect from any product that they purchase.

The range of stores that we have looked at demonstrates how versatile Magento can be. The different designs we have seen show (thanks to Magento's flexibility) that it is possible to differentiate our store from other stores, and vastly improve upon the default themes that are provided with Magento.

By learning how to theme your Magento store, you can open up the possibilities of creating an even better eCommerce store!

Summary

We've now introduced Magento, having:

- Seen what Magento is
- Seen what Magento can do
- Taken a look at existing Magento skin designs

We can now begin to take a look at Magento skins and begin customizing your online store!

2
Exploring Magento Themes

We've taken a look at what Magento is capable of, and examined some existing Magento themes, including the default theme displayed after installation. To begin theming Magento, we need to look at what a theme is made of.

What makes a Magento theme?

A Magento theme consists of three things:

1. XML **layout** files: They specify how the design is laid out.
2. PHTML **templates**: It is a mixture of PHP and HTML files, which specify how specific elements (for example, the shopping cart) of a layout look.
3. **Skins**: They provide the **Cascading Style Sheets** (CSS), and the images needed for creating the desired look for your Magento skin.

Interfaces and themes

The meaning of the terms theme and interface in Magento Commerce are contrasting.

Interfaces in Magento

An **interface** in Magento consists of *one or more* themes that together make up what you see in your store, as well as what it looks like to your customers. As we will see, Magento supports more than one theme at a time, so an interface is not necessarily just one theme.

Themes in Magento

A **theme** in Magento is what defines the look and feel of a store. Interfaces can have multiple themes assigned to them in Magento, enabling seasonal images to be used during certain periods, such as Christmas or Thanksgiving (in America).

A theme is what contains the layouts, templates, and skins, which we'll come to later in this chapter.

Locales in Magento

For multi-lingual Magento stores, themes can also contain locales, which is a translation of the copy (or content) of that particular store.

Default and non-default themes

Just to add to the confusion, there are also two types of themes: Default themes and non-default themes.

Default themes

A **default theme** in Magento is the primary theme of an interface. Magento looks for this default theme, and will load it to your store's frontend (that is the part that your customers see).

The default theme must contain all of the elements that the visitor will encounter when they visit our store, such as the shopping cart, checkout process, and so on. If your theme does not make use of these elements, then you don't need to include these elements in your default theme.

Non-default themes

A **non-default** theme allows you to create seasonal-looking online stores by applying as many or as few additional design elements, such as CSS or images, as you need. Non-default themes can also be used to customize your store to:

- Create a different look or layout for certain product pages, which require less (or more) information than normal products.

- Provide a way to display new products or even products that are "coming soon" without allowing customers to add them to their carts.

- Customize certain aspects of your store for country-specific requirements like customers expecting a button in a different position on the web site in a country.

Hierarchy of themes

As you can have multiple themes in Magento, there is a hierarchy for themes in place so that you can predict which themes will be displayed with a scheme of inheritance. The default theme provides a base for every aspect of your Magento store, from how it looks to where things are displayed. Subsequent themes can then overwrite what the default theme tells Magento, and any elements that are not overwritten are inherited from the default theme.

The default theme is always the lowest level theme in Magento's hierarchy. This means that non-default themes will simply overwrite what the default theme provides Magento with.

Skins, layouts, and templates

Skins, layouts, and templates are what Magento needs in a theme. Each of these helps to change a Magento theme in some way. Changing the skin changes the look and feel of your store, while changing the templates and layouts will change how the store is displayed, and what is displayed in it.

Skins

Skins within a Magento theme are what make the theme look the way it does. Skins specify colours, typefaces, and some layout rules, courtesy of CSS files and images. Your Magento theme's skin can also include JavaScript files to change your store's behavior.

Magento skins include files that affect your store's color scheme and logos.
The default Magento theme is shown in the following screenshot:

With some quite extensive changes to the skin elements of the Magento theme, our store can be made to look more like Magento's modern theme.

As you can see, the skin elements of a Magento theme offer a lot of flexibility in creating different visual impacts.

Layouts and blocks

The layout of the various views in Magento, such as, the shopping cart, product detail pages, and product results page, are controlled by the layout files. Magento's layout files are written in Extensible Markup Language (XML).

Layouts are also used to add, remove, and manipulate elements in *views* of your Magento store. By manipulating layout files, you can:

- Include JavaScript files in certain pages
- Include additional CSS files
- Remove content blocks, such as the shopping cart or callouts from particular pages

As an example, see the default Magento theme at
`http://demo.magentocommerce.com`:

This theme relies on a three-column layout, where a central column is used for the primary content of the page, and the two supplementary columns are used for additional comments. The products page use a two-column layout, and this change is achieved by changing the theme's layout files.

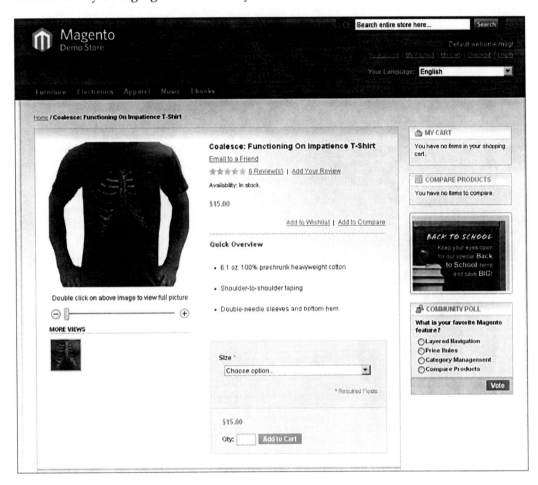

There are two types of blocks in Magento:

1. **Content blocks** produce the code within each structural block, and these use Magento's template files to generate the relevant information that is required for each block.

2. **Structural blocks** specify the structure of the page, such as the header, the content areas, and the footers.

A layout makes use of both types of blocks, as do templates in Magento.

Templates

As mentioned before, Magento **templates** specify what is to be displayed in each block of content in the form of content blocks. Template files are in PHTML.

The PHP in these template files is solely for the presentational logic, that is, the PHP is used only to make visual changes to your store in the template files. However, it doesn't affect the operation of the store itself, for example, calculating the cost of items in a shopping cart.

In Magento's default theme, a structural block comprises of an element of your store such as the shopping cart, a poll, or the page's main content, which is highlighted in the following screenshot:

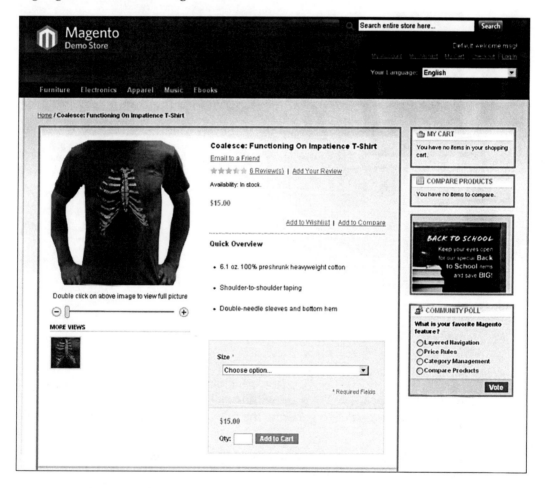

Templates in Magento are split into two different types. Firstly, there are **skeleton templates** that provide an overall structure for a page, such as one-column, two-column, and three-column layouts. Secondly, templates provide the HTML for the content blocks for each of the features that were highlighted earlier.

By handling templates this way, Magento further separates the templates' content from the layout of the store, allowing easier changes to either the template or the layout, without you needing to worry about one affecting the other.

Summary

In this chapter, we've looked at:

- The definitions used in the Magento system, including:
    - Interfaces
    - Themes
    - Default themes
    - Non-default themes
- The components of a Magento theme:
    - Skins — the CSS and images needed to create the look and feel of the Magento theme
    - Layouts, in XML
    - Templates, in PHTML

We can now begin to take a look at Magento's themes, as well as customizing your online store.

3
Magento Themes: The Basics

Now that we have a clearer idea of what a Magento theme is, we can begin designing a new theme for our new store. In this chapter, we'll cover the basics of Magento theme design and starting an online shop, including:

- Changing the store's logo to your own company's logo
- Removing the *callout* banners that come with the default Magento theme
- Altering an existing Magento theme's color scheme to suit your business' needs
- Setting your new Magento theme as the default theme for your store

Our case study: Cheesy Cheese Store

Cheesy Cheese Store wants a simple, customized theme for its new Magento store. Though there are plenty of cheese shops online, most of them are tailored for the more mature, conservative customer. Cheesy Cheese Store will be targeted at the younger cheese-eater that belongs to the well-exposed 18 - 24 age group.

What we need to consider design-wise

As with any e-commerce web site, there are a few fundamental elements that we'll require. They are as follows:

- Your store's logo.
- The shopping cart.
- The ability for customers to log in to view the status of their previous orders
- A search feature.
- Navigational elements to help visitors reach each page of your store easily. This includes links to your store's refund policy and terms of business, which are usually located in a web site's footer.
- Sufficient planning to take in to account the products that will be sold at the store, and the best ways to display these, both as individual products and as groups of products. The groups of products will be used for the product category pages and the search results page of your store.

All of these factors need to be accounted for when we design our Magento store.

Blank Theme from Magento Connect

A **Blank Theme** is a simplified Magento theme with very minimal graphics included. The Blank Theme allows for easier customization of your store, as it does not contain unnecessary graphics or any other elements. It is a Magento theme in its simplest form.

Accessing the Blank Theme

To use the **Blank Theme**, you will need an extension key to allow Magento to install it. You can get the extension key for free from Magento Connect at `http://www.magentocommerce.com/extension/518/blank-theme`. In order to see the extension key, click on the **Get extension key** button, located below the screenshot of the theme.

Once you have clicked on this, a box will appear asking you to accept the extensions license agreement.

Once you have read and accepted this agreement, click on the **Get Extension Key** button, and you will be presented with a text box containing the Blank Theme's extension key.

To install the theme, we need to remember (or copy and paste) the value in the text box, and open Magento's administration panel.

 Your browser will need JavaScript enabled in order to be able to access the Extension Key.

Magento's administration panel can usually be found by going to the /admin path wherever your Magento is installed. For example, if Magento is installed at http://example.com/magento, then your administration panel can be found at http://example.com/magento/admin.

Clearing Magento's cache

To make sure that we can see the changes we make to our theme, we need to disable Magento's cache. This will prevent our changes from being hidden by an older version of the theme that Magento is saving. We can disable the cache from the administration panel, under **System | Cache Management**.

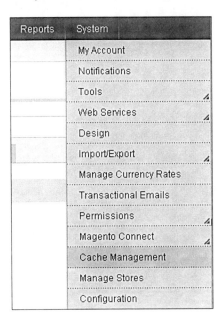

Select the **Disable** value from the drop-down list of values for **All Cache**, and save the page. Magento's cache is now disabled!

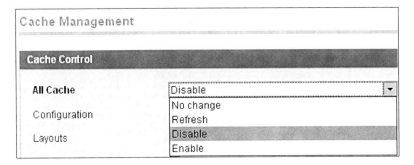

Installing Magento's Blank Theme

To install Magento's Blank Theme, ensure that you are still logged in to your administration panel, and select **System | Magento Connect | Magento Connect Manager**.

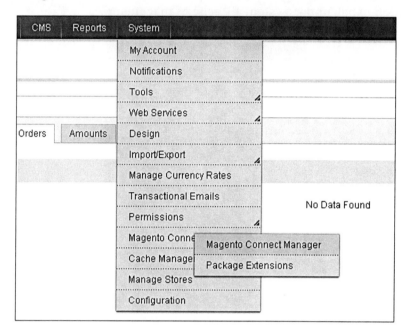

To use Magento Connect in the admin panel, all of the directories in your Magento installation will need full read, write, and execute permissions for all of the user groups, so that new extensions can be installed properly.

Magentoconnect MANAGER

Extensions   Settings

Return to Admin   Log Out

Install New Extensions

1   Search for modules via Magento Connect.

2   Paste extension key to install: [   ]   [Install]

Manage Existing Extensions   [Check for Upgrades]

Channel: connect.magentocommerce.com/core   [Commit Changes]

Clear all sessions after successfull install or upgrade: ☐

Package Name	Installed	Actions	Summary
Interface_Frontend_Default_Blank	1.1.8 (stable)	[▾]	This is a sample skeleton theme for Magento designers.
Lib_Google_Checkout	1.1.1 (stable)	[▾]	Google Checkout Library
Lib_Js_Calendar	1.1.7 (stable)	[▾]	Javascript Calendar for Magento
Lib_Js_Mage	1.1.3 (stable)	[▾]	Javascript Libraries for Magento
Lib_Js_Prototype	1.1.3 (stable)	[▾]	Prototype and Scriptaculous Javascript Libraries for Magento
Lib_Varien	1.1.3 (stable)	[▾]	Varien Library
Lib_ZF	1.1.1 (stable)	[▾]	Zend Framework
Lib_ZF_Locale	1.1.1 (stable)	[▾]	Zend Framework Locale
Mage_Core_Modules	1.1.8 (stable)	[▾]	Collection of Magento Core Modules

[Commit Changes]

If you don't set the proper permissions on the directories in which Magento needs to install the new theme, then you'll get an error, as shown in the following screenshot:

Magentoconnect MANAGER

Check Write Permissions

Error: Please check for sufficient write file permissions

Your Magento folder does not have sufficient write permissions, which this web based downloader requires.

If you wish to proceed downloading Magento packages online, please set all Magento folders to have writable permission for the web server user (example: apache) and press the "Refresh" button to try again.

Refresh

To learn more about setting write permissions, please visit the Magento community site for further details.

Changing your directories' permissions

One way to change your directory's permissions is with an FTP program, as described in Magento's installation process at http://www.magentocommerce.com/wiki/magento_installation_guide.

Making a theme Magento's default theme

To change the current theme to the blank theme, you now need to go back to the admin area of your Magento store, which you can do by clicking on the **Return to Admin** link at the top right of the screen.

Once in your store's admin panel, you can change the theme to the new **Blank Theme**, which we've just downloaded by selecting the **System | Configuration** option from the navigation panel.

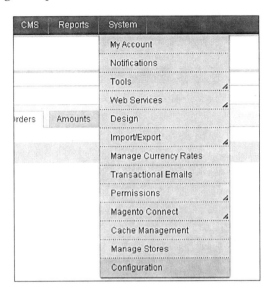

After this, select the **Design** option from the menu to the left.

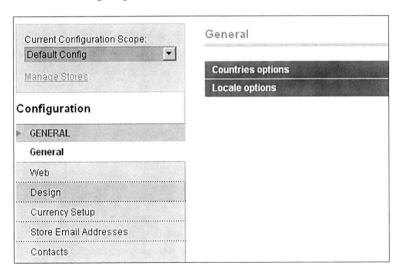

Once you're in the design configuration area of your Magento store's control panel, you will need to enter the new values for the theme for **Templates, Skin, Layout,** and **Default** values. Each of these values needs to be changed to blank in order to enable Magento to display the new theme.

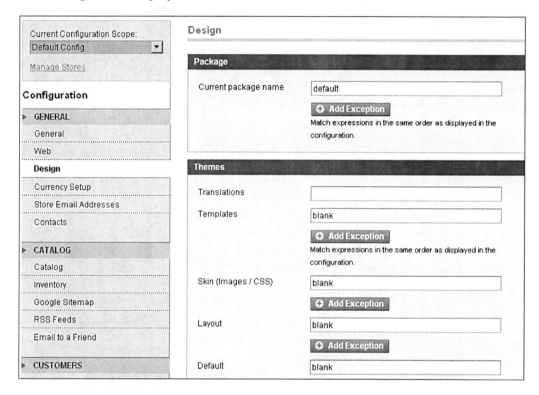

Now, if you select the **Save Config** button in the top right of your screen, then you should be able to view the blank theme in use on your Magento store.

What the Blank Theme looks like

Now that the Blank Theme is installed, we can view it on our Magento store's frontend. We can do this by closing our store's administration panel, and returning to the root of your Magento installation. So, if your store's administration panel is http://example.com/magento/admin, then you will need to go to http://example.com/magento to see the new theme.

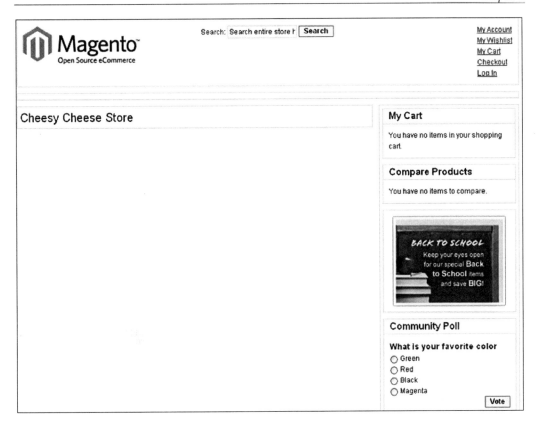

We don't have any content in our Magento store at the moment, so the home page looks a little bare. We can add the content to the home page through Magento's Content Management System.

Adding content with Magento's CMS

To access Magento's **Content Management System** (CMS), we need to log in to Magento's administration panel (at /admin within your Magento installation) again. From the **CMS** option, select the **Manage Pages** option in the navigation panel.

From the list of pages, select the page with the **Identifier** of **home**.

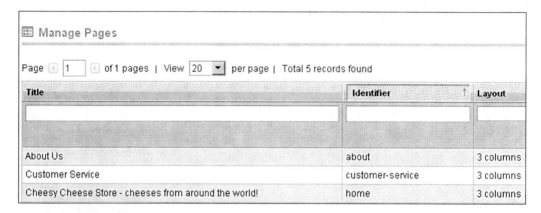

We can insert content formatted with HTML in to our store's home page from here.

Once the page is saved, we can return to the frontend of the store in order to see the content that we've just added (for example, `http://example.com/magento/` rather than `http://example.com/magento/admin`).

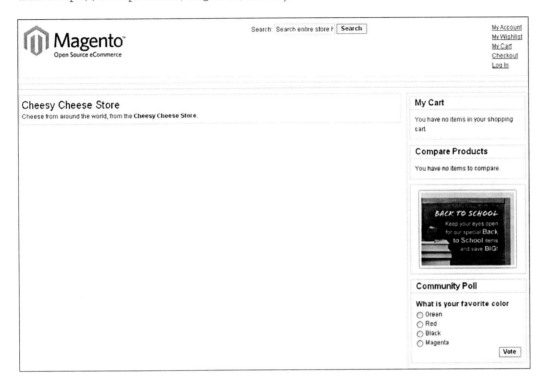

We can make our store's home page more interesting, by adding a graphic to promote our product.

If we save this image as `cheese-homepage.png` in the theme's skin directory (for example, `http://example.com/magento/frontend/default/blank/images/`), then we can use it on our store's home page by inserting the following HTML in to the content block of the home page within Magento's Content Management System:

```
<h1>Cheesy Cheese Store</h1>
<p>
   Cheese from around the world, from the
   <strong>Cheesy Cheese Store</strong>.
</p>
<img
   src = "http://example.com/magento/skin/frontend/default/blank/
images/cheese-homepage.png" alt="Cheesy Cheese Store - delicious
cheese!" />
```

Once this page is saved, refreshing our store's home page shows the new graphic.

 In order to see the changes, you will need to disable Magento's cache!

For ease, we'll keep the same layout for our new store for now, adding our own flair to the theme. Here, we'll introduce the Cheesy Cheese Store's new theme.

As you can see, a very noticeable difference can be achieved. The logo and space ship graphics are targeted towards our audience of younger cheese-eaters, and the colors are a lot more appealing than they were previously.

Cheesy Cheese Store's Magento theme

This makes it incredibly easy for us to start customizing Magento ourselves. There are just a few steps that we need to take in order to create our own basic Magento theme. The steps are:

- Changing your store's design
- Changing your store's logo
- Removing the callouts

Changing your store's design

To change the store's color scheme to match our original design for the Cheesy Cheese Store, we need to edit the `styles.css` file in the `skin/frontend/default/blank/css/` directory again.

The header

The next thing we can do is change the background color and background image of the header, by editing the style associated with `.header`:

```
.header {
padding:10px; border:1px solid #ddd;
}
```

We can change the background color and image by adding the following code to the CSS:

```
.header {
background: #333 url("../images/body_bg.png") top left no-repeat;
padding:10px; border:1px solid #ddd;
}
```

The background of our store should now be dark gray, but the image won't appear until we upload it to the right directory, `skin/frontend/default/blank/images/`. Our store's header should now look like this:

The search form

The search form in the header is our next element to style. We'll keep it centred, according to our design for Cheesy Cheese Store. The HTML for the form is quite straight forward, and allows us to identify what we need to style in the CSS:

```
<form id="search_mini_form"
    action="http://www.yourstore.com/magento/index.php/catalogsearch/
    result/" method="get">
  <fieldset class="form-search">
      <legend>Search Site</legend>
      <label for="search">Search:</label>
      <input id="search" type="text" class="input-text" name="q"
        value="" />
```

```
<button type="submit"
  class="button"><span>Search</span></button>
<div id="search_autocomplete"
    class="search-autocomplete"></div>
<script type="text/javascript">
   //<![CDATA[
   var searchForm = new Varien.searchForm('search_mini_form',
       'search', 'Search entire store here...');
   searchForm.initAutocomplete('http://www.yourstore.com
       /magento/index.php/catalogsearch/ajax/suggest/',
       'search_autocomplete');
   //]]>
</script>
</fieldset>
</form>
```

 A tool such as Firebug for Firefox can be useful to view the HTML behind Magento, but the View Source function, which is available in most browsers, can be equally useful.

We'll hide the label for the search form and restyle the submit button `.button`, by adding a new style to the `styles.css` template:

```
.header label {display: none}
.header .button {background: #FFFF00}
```

Our search form should now look more integrated with the header.

User links

The next elements that we can style are the user links in the header, which are grouped in an unordered list of class `.links`.

They're currently not very clear, but we can solve this with a little CSS.

```
header .links a {color: #FFF}
```

As you can see, they're now easier to read for our store's visitors.

Styling pages

We can style the main page content quite simply, by looking for the following CSS:

```
/* Base Columns */
col-left { float:left; width:230px; border:1px solid #ddd;
          padding:5px 5px 0; }
col-main { float:left; width:736px; border:1px solid #ddd;
          padding:5px; }
col-right { float:right; width:230px; border:1px solid #ddd;
          padding:5px 5px 0; }
```

We'll remove the border from each of these, and give them our newer background color (dark gray), and make sure that all of the content can be seen, by making the `fore-color` white.

```
/* Base Columns */
col-left, .col-main, .col-right
{background: #333;color: #FFF}
col-left {float:left; width:230px; padding:5px 5px 0; }
col-main {float:left; width:736px; padding:5px; }
col-right {float:right; width:230px; padding:5px 5px 0; }
```

Our store's primary content area now looks like this:

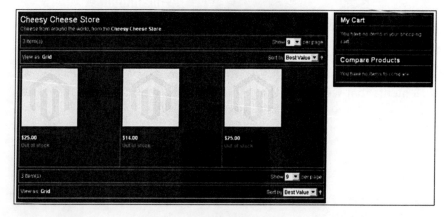

Note that we need to style links too, which we can do with the following CSS:

```
col-left a, .col-main a, .col-right a {color: #FFF}
```

We'll also hide the *out of stock* message that appears, since we're not using Magento to track Cheesy Cheese Store's stock at the moment. To do this, we simply add this CSS to the `styles.css` file:

```
span.out-of-stock {display: none}
```

Lastly, change the **Add to Wishlist** and **Add to Compare** links to tidy things up a little, making them smaller and less obvious, because the product itself should be more of a focus.

```
ul.add-to-links li {display: inline}
ul.add-to-links li a {color: #DDD;font-size: 90%}
```

Our page content now looks a lot smarter:

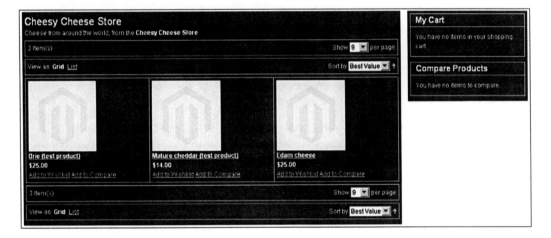

Styling your store's footer

The footer is relatively easy to style, though the HTML is a bit verbose:

```
<div class="footer">
  <ul>
    <li>
    <a href="http://www.yourdomain.com/magento/index.php/
            about-magento-demo-store">About Us</a></li>
    <li class="last">
      <a href="http://www.yourdomain.com/magento/index.php/
            customer-service">Customer Service</a></li>
  </ul>
  <ul class="links">
```

```
        <li class="first">
          <a href="http://www.yourdomain.com/magento/index.php/catalog/
              seo_sitemap/category/" title="Site Map" >Site Map</a>
        </li>
        <li>
          <a href="http://www.yourdomain.com/magento/index.php/
            atalogsearch/term/popular/" title="Search Terms" >
              Search Terms</a>
        </li>
  <li>
          <a href="http://www.yourdomain.com/magento/index.php/
            catalogsearch/advanced/" title="Advanced Search" >
                Advanced Search</a>
        </li>
        <li class="last">
          <a href="http://www.yourdomain.com/magento/index.php/
                  contacts/"  title="Contact Us" >Contact Us</a>
        </li>
      </ul>
      <p>Help Us to Keep Magento Healthy –
        <a href="http://www.magentocommerce.com/bug-tracking"
          onclick="this.target='_blank'">
        <strong>Report All Bugs</strong></a> (ver. 1.1.8)
      </p>
      <address>&copy; Richard Carter</address>
    </div>
```

We don't want links to the *customer service* or *about* pages in the Cheesy Cheese Store, so we'll remove these. To do this, we need to log in to our Magento store's administration panel, and select the **Static Blocks** option under the **CMS** navigation option. Select the **footer_links** static block, set its status to **disabled**, and select the **Save Block** option.

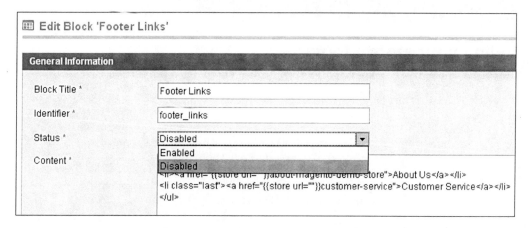

Now, these links will not be displayed in the footer. As for the other links, we can style these with CSS and apply it to the `.footer .list`, but first we'll style the `.footer div` itself. Currently it reads:

```
.footer { border:1px solid #ddd; padding:10px; }
```

To style it like the rest of our store, we'll remove the border and add a background color again:

```
.footer {
  background: #333;
  color: #FFF;
  padding:10px;
}
```

We'll also style the links in the footer to ensure that they're visible:

```
.footer a {color: #FFF}
```

Our store's footer is now styled.

Styling the product pages

Now that the homepage is styled, there are just a few changes left that we need to make to style the product pages in the same way, and to create a consistent look across our Magento store. The first is the breadcrumbs div tag, `.breadcrumbs`, which currently appears white.

This is quickly fixed by adding the breadcrumbs class to our existing CSS:

```
.breadcrumbs,
.col-left, .col-main, .col-right
{background: #333;color: #FFF}
```

The link color in the breadcrumb is also in need of some CSS:

```
.breadcrumbs a,
.col-left a, .col-main a, .col-right a {color: #FFF}
```

The breadcrumb is now styled like the rest of the store.

Changing the Magento store's logo

One of the most obvious things that we can do to customize our Magento store is to change the logo to our own. To change the store's logo, in the Magento admin panel, go to the **Design** section under the **Configuration** option in the **System** menu.

Once you're on the page, select the **Header** section.

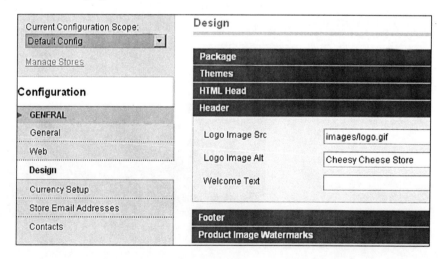

From here, you can change your logo file and the text used if the logo isn't displayed. It's useful to search engines if you set this to be the name of your store (in our case, Cheesy Cheese Store).

The logo itself is stored in the `/skin/frontend/default/blank/images/` directory, which is where you'll need to upload your new logo file. For Cheesy Cheese Store our logo file looks like this:

We'll save the logo file as `logo2.gif`, and set the transparency color to the gray in the background, so that eventually the stars will be able to shine through the logo. We now need to save the new value for the logo's name (that is, replace `logo.gif` with `logo2.gif`, or whatever name you have given your new logo).

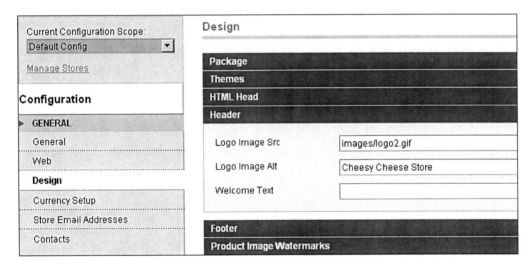

If we refresh our Magento store, then we should now be able to see the new logo.

As our new logo is larger than the old Magento store logo, we need to edit some CSS, which we can find in the `skin/frontend/default/blank/css/` directory of our Magento installation. Locate the CSS in the `styles.css` file that reads:

```
.logo {
    float:left; width:200px; height:63px; overflow:hidden;
}
```

We need to remove the `overflow: hidden` declaration, and change the height and width values to the height and width of our new logo:

```
.logo {
    float:left; width:122px; height:109px;
}
```

We also need to change the dimensions of the logo's link so that our store's visitors can still click on the logo to return to the store's home page. The CSS for this is a few lines under the declaration of `.logo`:

```
.header .logo a {
    display:block; width:175px; height:200px;
}
```

These values need changing to those below for our new logo, which is 122 pixels wide and 109 pixels high:

```
.header .logo a {
    display:block; width:122px; height:109px;
}
```

The full logo should now be visible (though it'll look a little odd since it's aliased for a darker background color).

Changing your store's favicon

One touch many designers forget about is the store's **favicon**: The little icon usually displayed next to your browser's address bar, and stored in your browser's bookmarked web site. The default favicon in Magento is the Magento logo, scaled to a smaller size:

A good favicon is usually:

- Recognisable at a small size: A favicon is 16 by 16 pixels in size
- Related to your logo or store's products

Of course, these are just suggestions. Rules are there to be broken, but it's worthwhile keeping the theme of your favicon close to the theme of your store's products. On this basis, we'll change Cheesy Cheese Store's favicon from the default Magento icon to this cheese-related favicon.

The favicon file for our theme is located in the `/skin/frontend/default/default/` directory of your Magento installation, and is called `favicon.ico`.

Creating a favicon file

There are a number of online tools that allow you to create favicon files, including Dynamic Drive's Favicon Generator (`http://tools.dynamicdrive.com/favicon/`).

Removing the callouts

Callouts are graphic advertisments embedded in most Magento themes by default to allow you to promote certain products on your store. For example, in our blank theme, a callout is displayed below the shopping cart and compare features, in the righthand column.

Of course, you can customize these graphics in the way that you want, but as the Cheesy Cheese Store is in need of a simple theme, we'll remove them.

Callout graphics

The callout graphics are stored in the `skin/frontend/default/` `blank/images/media/` directory of your Magento installation (assuming your theme is called **blank**).

To remove the callout graphics from our store's theme, we need to edit a layout file called `catalog.xml`, which is located in `app/design/frontend/default/` `blank/layout/`.

Removing the callouts on the righthand side

To remove the callouts in the righthand columns of the Magento theme, you'll need to find the following code in the `catalog.xml` file, and comment out or remove the highlighted code below:

```
<reference name="right">
  <block type="core/template" before="cart_sidebar"
    name="catalog.compare.sidebar"
    template="catalog/product/compare/sidebar.phtml"/>
  <block type="core/template" name="right.permanent.callout"
    template="callouts/right_col.phtml"/>
</reference>
```

The code should now be:

```
<reference name="right">
  <block type="core/template" before="cart_sidebar"
    name="catalog.compare.sidebar"
    template="catalog/product/compare/sidebar.phtml"/>
  <!--
    <block type="core/template" name="right.permanent.callout"
    template="callouts/right_col.phtml"/>
  -->
</reference>
```

Removing callouts on the lefthand side

Locate the following block of code:

```
<block type="core/template" name="left.permanent.callout"
    template="callouts/left_col.phtml">
  <action method="setImgSrc">
    <src>images/media/col_left_callout.jpg</src>
```

```
      </action>
      <action method="setImgAlt" translate="alt" module="catalog">
        <alt>Our customer service is available 24/7. Call us at (800)
          DEMO-NUMBER.</alt>
      </action>
      <action method="setLinkUrl">
        <url>checkout/cart</url>
      </action>
    </block>
```

To remove the callouts, you can either remove the code above or comment it out, in the same way you would comment HTML out:

```
<!--
    <block type="core/template" name="left.permanent.callout"
      template="callouts/left_col.phtml">
    <action
      method="setImgSrc"><src>images/media/col_left_callout.jpg
    </src></action>
    <action method="setImgAlt" translate="alt"
        module="catalog"><alt>Our customer service is available 24/7
        . Call us at (800) DEMO-NUMBER.</alt></action>
    <action method="setLinkUrl"><url>checkout/cart</url></action>
    </block>
  -->
```

Now, if you save and upload the file to your server, you should see then that the callouts displayed on the right and lefthand columns have gone.

Displaying featured products on the home page

Many stores show featured products on their home page, and this is something that we can do in Magento too.

Creating a "featured" category

One of the easiest ways to display featured products on your store's home page is to create a category containing the products that you want to feature, and display the contents of this category on your store's home page. To create a new category, select the **Catalog | Manage Categories** option from the administration panel's menu:

Select the **Add Root Category** button on the left, and create a **New Category** named **Featured products**. Be sure to set the value for **Is Active** to **No**: This means that the category won't be displayed elsewhere on the store.

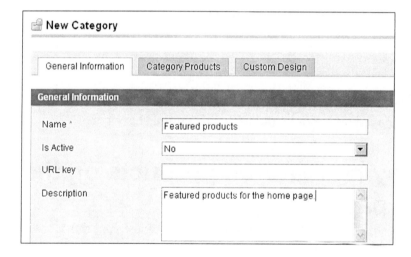

Once you have saved your category, make a note of its ID, which is displayed in a bracket to the right of the category's name:

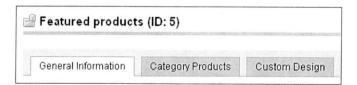

In earlier versions of Magento, you had to study the URL of the category in the administration panel. For example, if it ends with `/edit/5`, then the category's ID is 5.

To assign a product to this category, select a product from your store (or create a product if you have not yet done so), and go to the **Categories** tab to its left. You can check the **Featured products** category we just created here:

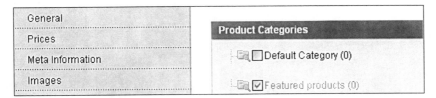

Displaying the "featured" category through the Content Management System

To display featured products on the home page, remain logged in to your store's administration panel (usually at `http://example.com/magento/admin`), and go back to the Content Management System. Select **CMS** and then **Manage Pages** from the menu.

Select your store's home page again. Do you remember the ID of the featured category we created? This is where we need to use it, while inserting the featured products below our introductory text:

```
<h1>Cheesy Cheese Store</h1>
<p>
   Cheese from around the world, from the <strong>Cheesy Cheese
      Store</strong>.
</p>
{{block type="catalog/product_list" category_id="5"
      template="catalog/product/list.phtml"}}
```

Once the page is saved, refresh your store's home page (for example, `http://example.com/magento`), and any products that are associated with the featured products category will be displayed:

Cheesy Cheese Store so far

Our store now looks more interesting than it did with the default Magento themes, and is tailored towards our store's most likely customers. If you chose not to display featured products on your homepage, as above, your homepage will now look similar to this:

There's still plenty that we can do to style and customize our Magento store, and it's this attention to detail that makes web designing so interesting.

Summary

We've covered the basics of theme design for Magento, as well as things to consider before you start a new e-commerce business, including:

- Installing a theme from Magento Connect
- Basic techniques for styling your Magento store, including changing your logo and changing the colors of your store
- Changing your Magento store's favicon file

In the next chapter, we'll be looking at altering the layout of your Magento store, and advanced techniques for changing your store's theme.

Magento Theme Layout

We've learned how to change the basics of our new Magento theme, including changing the colors, and styling the major elements of your store. But we can do much more to customize Magento. In this chapter, we'll:

- Review what a layout in Magento is, and what it can do
- Change layouts with Magento's CMS
- Alter layouts using the XML layout provided by Magento

Themes and Layouts in Magento

A layout is an element of a theme in Magento. A theme consists of:

- **Skins**: They comprise of the CSS and images that define the look of your Magento store
- **Templates**: These define what each block contains in your store
- **Layouts**: They define what is displayed where in your Magento store
- **Locales**: These are optional elements that allow your store to be presented in multiple languages

We've already changed some of our new store's skin elements, like changing the colors of the store's elements. We can now use layouts to change where everything is displayed in relation to each other. There are two ways you can change your store's layout:

1. On a page-per-page basis, if the page is controlled through Magento's CMS.
2. Through layout files, by applying the layout change to any number of pages within your Magento store .

We'll look at changing the layout of our Cheesy Cheese Store using both these methods.

Changing our store's layout with CMS

Let's take a look at how we can use a layout to change our store. The Blank Theme that we installed and altered for our store has a number of built-in layouts, which we can make use of to customize our store, including one column, two column, and three column layout options. One of the simplest ways we can change our store's layout is with Magento's CMS.

Log in to your Magento store's administration panel and select **CMS** | **Manage Pages**:

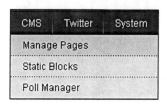

Select the page's layout that you wish to change. We'll change the layout of Cheesy Cheese Store's **About Us** page:

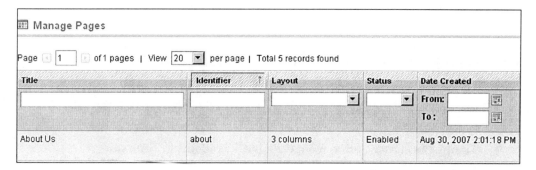

As we can see, the layout of this page is currently set to **3 columns**. If we select this page from the list, then we are presented with options to change the page's content. Now, if we select the **Custom Design** tab to the left of the screen, then we can change the page's configuration by selecting a new value from the **Layout** drop-down box. We'll change the page's **Layout** to **2 columns with right bar**.

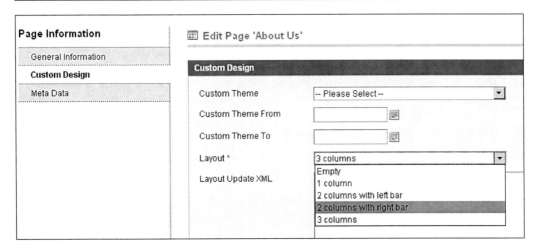

Once this page is saved, we should be able to see the result of a change in the layout. If we go to the frontend of our store (not the administration panel), and view the **About Us** page, we can see:

Different column, different content

As the lefthand and righthand side columns are stored in different template files in Magento, the content that appears in the lefthand column is now different from that of the righthand column. You can change this by editing the layout file, which is located in `app/design/frontend/default/blank/layout/catalog.xml`.

Template path hints

In order to help us alter our store's layout, we can enable template path hints. These hints allow you to see the paths (addresses) of each block's templates in Magento, and can be useful when theming Magento, particularly when you are altering the layout.

Enabling template path hints

You can enable template path hints from the **System | Configuration** selection of your Magento store's administration panel:

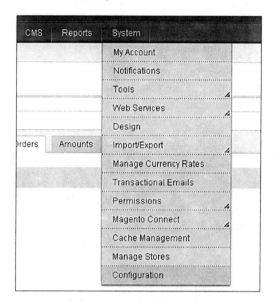

From here, you will need to select the store that you'd like to change from the list at the top left of the screen. Here, we'll choose **Main Website**, or whatever your Magento store is called:

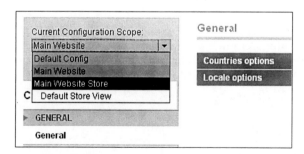

Once the page has reloaded, select the **Developer** tab towards the bottom of the page:

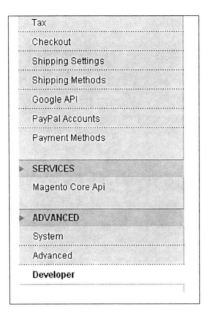

You should now be able to see **Template Path Hints** under the **Debug** section of the page. Change this value from **No** to **Yes** to turn template path hints on:

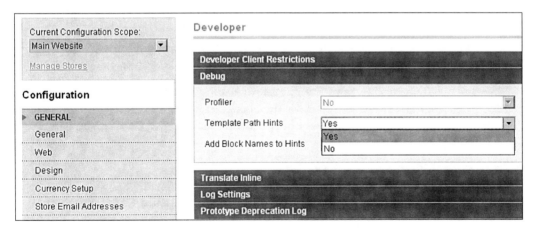

Saving this new configuration will now display path hints beside each of the templates in Magento, making it easier to work out how changes to the layout will affect your store's look. Now that the template path hints are activated, our store's frontend will have changed a little:

Layout terminology in Magento

Within a Magento layout, you can assign content blocks to structural blocks. If you recall, a structural block effectively positions the content within the page, while a content block provides the actual content within the page, whether it is a category list, callout, or the basket.

Within the layout XML files of your Magento store, there are three important elements:

1. **Handles**: They provide means of identifying a particular view within your store.

2. **Blocks**: They determine the visual structure and the behavior of each of the elements in your store's pages. Within a block element in the layout XML, there are a number of attributes that we can use.

3. **References**: They allow the layout files to reference one another, which means that one block can contain another block in Magento.

In Magento, each module defines the layout for itself. For example, the checkout.xml file defines the layout for the checkout module, whereas the customer.xml file defines the layout of Magento's customer account module.

A brief guide to XML

Layout files in Magento make use of XML. It can be baffling to see XML for the first time, especially if you're not familiar with XHTML. However, the markup is quite simple once you're used to it.

There is one simple rule in creating a well-formed XML document: Every element must close. An element in XML can close in two ways.

1. The element can self-close.
2. The element can be closed with a closing tag of its own type.

Self-closing elements in XML

A self-closing element in XML is an element that closes itself. Let us take, as an example, the XML element `<thing>`. If this element self-closed, it would look like this:

```
<thing />
```

Closing XML elements normally

The other way to close an XML element is with a closing tag of the opening tag's type. Therefore, with the `<thing>` tag, a valid XML element would look like this:

```
<thing>Value (if any)</thing>
```

Entity escapes in XML

Just as in HTML and XHTML, XML requires some characters to escape, in order to prevent data in the XML file from being misinterpreted. The characters that you'll need to watch out for in your XML file are:

Character	Description	Escape
&	Ampersand	&
<	Less than	<
>	Greater than	>
'	Apostrophe	'
"	Quotation mark	"

For example, if you wanted to display **A & B > C < D 'E' "F"** in our XML file, it would look like this:

```
A &amp; B &gt; C &lt; D &apos;E &apos; &quot;F &quot;
```

Now that we have a better grasp of XML, we can look more closely at changing the layout using Magento's XML layout.

Customizing Magento layouts with XML

We already have a two-column layout for the Cheesy Cheese Store, but what if we wanted the column displayed to the left, rather than the right of the content? Currently, the Cheesy Cheese Store has a column on the righthand side, which contains the shopping cart and recently viewed products:

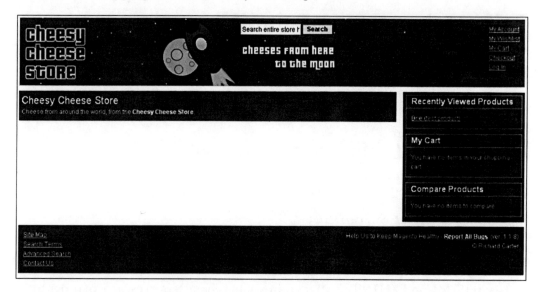

To change the column from the right to the lefthand side of our store, we need to locate the catalog.xml file in the app/design/frontend/default/blank/layout/ directory of our Magento store's installation.

Once the file has been opened, locate the opening <default> XML tag, which is the handle that identifies that the changes made to the layout here will impact upon most of the other pages in your Magento store. You should find the XML below nested within the <default> tag:

```
<default>
  <reference name="top.menu">
    <block type="catalog/navigation" name="catalog.topnav"
      template="catalog/navigation/top.phtml"/>
  </reference>
  <reference name="left">
    <!--<block type="core/template" name="left.permanent.callout"
      template="callouts/left_col.phtml">
```

```
      <action method="setImgSrc">
        <src>images/media/col_left_callout.jpg</src>
      </action>
      <action method="setImgAlt" translate="alt" module="catalog">
        <alt>Our customer service is available 24/7. Call us at (800)
          DEMO-NUMBER.</alt>
      </action>
      <action method="setLinkUrl">
        <url>checkout/cart</url>
      </action>
    </block>-->
  </reference>
  <reference name="left">
    <block type="core/template" before="cart_sidebar"
      name="catalog.compare.sidebar"
      template="catalog/product/compare/sidebar.phtml"/>
    <!--<block type="core/template" name="right.permanent.callout"
        template="callouts/right_col.phtml"/>-->
  </reference>
  <reference name="footer_links">
    <action method="addLink" translate="label title" module="catalog"
        ifconfig="catalog/seo/site_map">
      <label>Site Map</label>
      <url helper="catalog/map/getCategoryUrl" />
      <title>Site Map</title>
    </action>
  </reference>
</default>
```

We can tell Magento to use the left-hand column layout, by adding the code
highlighted below in to the XML file:

```
<default>
  <reference name="root">
    <action method="setTemplate"><template>page/2columns-
      left.phtml</template></action>
  </reference>
  <!-- more layout omitted -->
</default>
```

After uploading the new layout file, we'll be able to see that our column's content is now displayed on the left, rather than the right of the primary content:

Notice the callout template, which is highlighted above, is not displayed on the page, as we hid the callouts in our store earlier on.

Changes not showing up — Disable Magento's cache

If you cannot see your changes after refreshing the page, don't forget to disable Magento's cache in your administration panel, under **System | Cache Management**. You will probably want to re-enable Magento's cache once your store is ready to "go live".

Layout files' location

The layout files are located in the `app/design/frontend/default/blank/layout/` directory, rather than in the `skin/frontend` directory.

Remember that `default` is the interface name, while `blank` is our theme's name.

Handles

Handles in Magento layout files allow a particular view in your Magento store to be identified. If the handle is `<default>`, then almost every page in your Magento store is affected by the layout information.

Non-default handles

If the handle is not `<default>`, then the updates in the nested XML beneath it will only apply to the relevant page(s) in your Magento store.

Let's have a look at part of the `cms.xml` XML layout file from Magento:

```
<layout version="0.1.0">
  <default>
    <reference name="footer">
      <block type="cms/block" name="cms_footer_links"
            before="footer_links">
        <action method="setBlockId">
          <block_id>footer_links</block_id>
        </action>
      </block>
    </reference>
  </default>
  <cms_page>
    <reference name="content">
      <block type="cms/page" name="cms_page"/>
    </reference>
  </cms_page>
</layout>
```

The `<default>` handle applies a layout to any page which has its layout defined by the `cms.xml` file. The non-default handle in the layout above is `<cms_page>`, which controls the layout for pages created in Magento's CMS. The layout above simply tells Magento where to insert the page's content.

Useful handles in Magento

Some useful layout handles in Magento are the identifiers, which allow you to single out a particular page or section of your Magento store, such as the following:

XML handle	Page it identifies in Magento	XML layout file, which the XML handle is referenced in
`catalog_category_default`	The default view of a category of products.	`catalog.xml`
`customer_account`	The customer account page, shown when a customer is logged in to their account in your store.	`customer.xml`
`catalog_product_view`	The product page view (a page that displays an individual product).	`catalog.xml`
`cms_page`	Pages created with Magento's Content Management System.	`cms.xml`

There are many other handles available to you, and as Magento expands, these will change and evolve.

 As we're only wanting to theme Magento, we shouldn't have to change these handles (instead, we will be referencing them), but it's still useful to know what they do.

Using Magento layout: Another example

We can apply the three-column page template to our Magento store in a similar way to the two-column layout above, by overwriting the template with the three-column layout. Open the `catalog.xml` file in the `app/design/frontend/default/blank/layout/` directory, and find the XML mentioned below (assuming that you had previously set the layout to use the two-column layout):

```
<default>
<!-- Mage_Catalog -->
<reference name="root">
<action method="setTemplate">
<template>page/2columns-left.phtml</template>
</action>
</reference>
```

We can just change the reference within the `<template>` tags to `3columns.phtml`:

```
<reference name="root">
<action method="setTemplate">
<template>page/3columns.phtml</template>
</action>
</reference>
```

Once we've uploaded the newer layout file, refresh the page, and you should see that the home page is now divided into three columns:

As you can see, the other pages of the Cheesy Cheese Store also make use of the three-column layout, just like the **About Us** page:

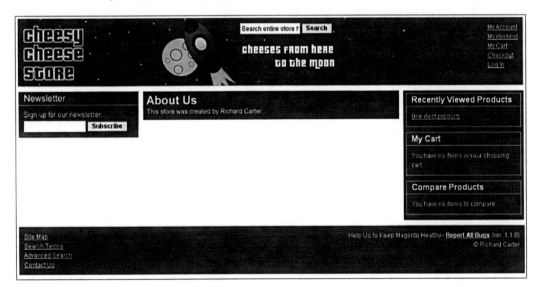

Changing the layout on a particular page

You can also change the layout on any one particular page, by making use of the setTemplate action within the relevant handle in the catalog.xml layout file.

If we want to change the product view page's layout to use the left-column layout, then we can change the following XML in `catalog.xml` under the `catalog_product_view` (non-default) handle:

```
<reference name="root">
  <action method="setTemplate">
    <template>page/2columns-right.phtml</template>
  </action>
</reference>
```

All that we need to change is the word `right` to `left`:

```
<reference name="root">
  <action method="setTemplate">
    <template>page/2columns-left.phtml</template>
  </action>
</reference>
```

Once the page is refreshed, the product view page will now be displayed with the column to the left.

Summary

This chapter has covered the basics of layouts, including:

- A detailed look at what layouts are in Magento, and what you can do with layouts
- Changing your store's layout using the CMS
- The basics of XML, the language of layouts in Magento
- Altering your store's layout with Magento's XML layout file

We'll start looking at more complex themes in Magento in the coming chapters, while building upon what we've learned and seen so far.

5
Non-default Magento Themes

We've made use of default themes in Magento, and we can customize our Magento store further by using non-default themes. In particular, we'll look at:

- Setting your non-default theme to be the one that your visitors will see
- Creating a number of simple non-default themes
- The theme hierarchy in Magento

Uses of non-default themes

Magento's flexibility in themes gives a lot of scope for possible uses of non-default themes. Along with the ability to have seasonal themes on our Magento store, non-default themes have a range of uses:

- A/B testing
- Easily rolled-back themes
- Changing the look and feel of specific pages, such as for a particular product within your store
- Creating brand-specific stores within your store, distinguishing your store's products further, if you sell a variety of the same products from different brands

A/B testing

A/B testing allows you to compare two different aspects of your store. You can test different designs on different weeks, and can then compare which design attracted more sales. Magento's support for non-default themes allows you to do this relatively easily.

Bear in mind that the results of such a test may not represent what actually drives your customers to buy your store's products for a number of reasons. True A/B testing on web sites is performed by presenting the different designs to your visitors at random. However, performing it this way may give you an insight in to what your customers prefer.

Easily rolled-back themes

If you want to make changes to your store's existing theme, then you can make use of a non-default theme to overwrite certain aspects of your store's look and feel, without editing your original theme.

This means that if your customers don't like a change, or a change causes problems in a particular browser, then you can simply roll-back the changes, by changing your store's settings to display the original theme.

Non-default themes

A **default theme** is the default look and feel to your Magento store. That is, if no other styling or presentational logic is specified, then the default theme is the one that your store's visitors will see. Magento's default theme looks similar to the following screenshot:

Non-default themes are very similar to the default themes in Magento. Like default themes, Magento's non-default themes can consist of one or more of the following elements:

- Skins—images and CSS
- Templates—the logic that inserts each block's content or feature (for example, the shopping cart) in to the page
- Layout—XML files that define where content is displayed
- Locale—translations of your store

The major difference between a default and a non-default theme in Magento is that a default theme must have all of the layout and template files required for Magento to run. On the other hand, a non-default theme does not need all of these to function, as it relies on your store's default theme, to some extent.

> **Locales in Magento**
>
> Many themes are already partially or fully translated into a huge variety of languages. Locales can be downloaded from the Magento Commerce website at `http://www.magentocommerce.com/langs`.

Magento theme hierarchy

In its current releases, Magento supports two themes: a default theme, and a non-default theme. The non-default theme takes priority when Magento is deciding what it needs to display. Any elements not found in the non-default theme are then found in the default theme specified.

> Future versions of Magento should allow more than one default theme to be used at a time, as well as allow more detailed control over the hierarchy of themes in your store.

Magento theme directory structure

Every theme in Magento must maintain the same directory structure for its files. As you may have seen in previous chapters, the skin, templates, and layout are stored in their own directories.

Templates

Templates are located in the `app/design/frontend/interface/theme/template` directory of your Magento store's installation, where `interface` is your store's interface (or package) name (usually `default`), and `theme` is the name of your theme (for example, `cheese`).

Templates are further organized in subdirectories by module. So, templates related to the catalog module are stored in `app/design/frontend/interface/theme/template/catalog/` directory, whereas templates for the checkout module are stored in `app/design/frontend/interface/theme/template/checkout` directory.

Layout

Layout files are stored in app/design/frontend/interface/theme/layout. The name of each layout file refers to a particular module. For example, catalog.xml contains layout information for the catalog module, whereas checkout.xml contains layout information for the checkout module.

Skins

Skins are not stored in Magento's app directory like templates and layout. They're stored in the skin/frontend/interface/theme/ directory.

Images are typically stored in the skin/frontend/interface/theme/images/ directory. Depending on the CSS used within your theme, your images could be contained within another directory.

CSS files are located in the skin/frontend/interface/theme/css/ directory, which typically includes your theme's print stylesheet, as well as stylesheets for your store's look and feel. Theme-specific JavaScript files are located in the skin/frontend/interface/theme/js/ directory.

 While the locations of these files can be altered in your theme's layout files, maintaining this structure will make your theme easier to use for other Magento theme designers familiar with other themes structured like this one.

If you don't use this structure in your theme, then Magento may not be able to find the elements that it is looking for, so your theme may not work as you expect!

 Remember that there's a difference between an interface and a theme in Magento. When we talk about themes, remember that a theme is a *part* of an interface (also known as a package).

Assigning your non-default theme

In order to be able to see the changes that the non-default theme will make to our store, we need to change the themes in Magento's administration panel. Log in to your Magento store's administration panel, and select the **System** tab in the navigation:

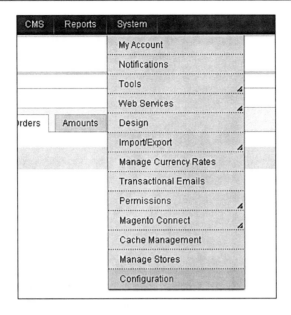

From here, select the **Design** tab under the **Configuration** option in the drop-down menu. Change the current configuration scope to whichever scope you want the changes to apply to. We'll use the **Default Config** scope:

For our first non-default theme example, we're just changing the header image, which comes under **Skin (Images/CSS)**. If the Christmas theme also changes the default theme's layout, then we would need to change the value of the **Layout** option to Christmas here too. Once you've saved the changes, the relevant elements of your non-default theme will be displayed.

Restrictions with assigning themes

This doesn't mean that you can't *have* more than one non-default theme stored on your Magento store—it simply means that you can only display one of these seasonal themes at a time. Future versions of Magento will have greater support for multiple themes.

Creating non-default themes

Unlike default themes, you don't need to create a copy of your default theme's files—you only have to change the files that you want to change.

Skin changes

If we wanted to change your Magento store's header image to tie in with Christmas, then you could create a non-default theme, which includes only one file, that is, the header image. Currently, the Cheesy Cheese Store's header looks like this:

As we want to keep the proportions of the store's design the same in the default and non-default themes, our new header image's proportions need to be kept the same. We also need to consider the legibility of the content which appears above this image, such as the options for your store's visitors to log in and manage their account.

Our new header image is themed to fit with the remainder of the web site, while giving a fresh look for the Christmas period.

After uploading the new header image in the relevant directory — `skin/frontend/` `default/christmas/images/`, we can see our new header image in our store's design:

No changes

If you can't see any changes, check that you have turned the system cache off, and make sure you've set the non-default theme to be used in Magento's administration panel!

This technique can be used for a huge variety of events throughout the year, including religious holidays, conferences, and events relevant to your store's audience. By taking the effort to update your Magento store for seasonal events, you can show your customers that your store is up-to-date and well-maintained, helping to reinforce the image of reliability in their eyes.

Template changes

To coincide with Christmas, we could create a Christmas-themed callout banner, advertising a special offer on shipping before a particular date. In the default Magento theme, one of the callouts was located beneath the cart, and product comparison features were in the righthand column of the store:

Clearly, this callout banner isn't suitable for our store. **BACK TO SCHOOL** discounts on cheese are unnecessary!

We previously hid the callouts. Therefore, to display them again, we need to edit the `catalog.xml` file in the `app/design/default/blank/layout/` directory. The callout is referenced in the following XML:

```
<reference name="right">
  <block type="core/template" before="cart_sidebar"
      name="catalog.compare.sidebar"
      template="catalog/product/compare/sidebar.phtml"/>
  <!--
  <block type="core/template" name="right.permanent.callout"
  template="callouts/right_col.phtml"/>
  -->
</reference>
```

By un-commenting this, we tell Magento that we want to display the callout graphic in our store's righthand column again:

```
<reference name="right">
  <block type="core/template" before="cart_sidebar"
      name="catalog.compare.sidebar"
      template="catalog/product/compare/sidebar.phtml"/>
  <block type="core/template" name="right.permanent.callout"
      template="callouts/right_col.phtml"/>
</reference>
```

Once we've saved this change and uploaded the `catalog.xml` layout file to our store, the callout graphic is displayed once again on the page. There are two ways in which we can change the callout graphic to suit our needs now:

1. By editing the callout image itself. This is stored at `skin/default/default/images/media/col_right_callout.jpg`.

2. By using the non-default theme we've created, "Christmas", to overwrite the callout image.

We'll use the non-default theme to display the callout image that we want on our store, without disturbing the default theme's images and code. This way, it is truly a 'seasonal' theme that can easily be replaced once the Christmas period is over.

We will need to upload our new callout graphic to the `skin/default/christmas/images/media/` directory, where `christmas` is the name of our non-default theme. We'll call the graphic itself `col_right_christmas.jpg`.

Callout graphic dimensions

If your theme is based upon the blank Magento theme available through Magento Connect (as the Cheesy Cheese Store's theme is), the maximum width for the callout graphics is 195 pixels.

Now, we need to create the template file that uses the righthand column callout graphic in our non-default theme. We can do this by copying the equivalent file in Magento's default theme, `app/design/frontend/default/default/template/callouts/right_col.phtml`, in to the same location within our non-default theme `app/design/frontend/default/christmas/template/callouts/right_col.phtml`.

You'll need to create a directory called "`christmas`" and its sub directories here.

The code currently looks like this (the code of interest to us is highlighted):

```php
<?php
/**
 * Magento
 *
 * NOTICE OF LICENSE
 *
 * This source file is subject to the Academic Free License (AFL
   3.0)
 * that is bundled with this package in the file LICENSE_AFL.txt.
 * It is also available through the world-wide-web at this URL:
 * http://opensource.org/licenses/afl-3.0.php
 * If you did not receive a copy of the license and are unable to
 * obtain it through the world-wide-web, please send an email
 * to license@magentocommerce.com so we can send you a copy
   immediately.
 *
 * DISCLAIMER
```

```
 *
 * Do not edit or add to this file if you wish to upgrade Magento to
   newer
 * versions in the future. If you wish to customize Magento for your
 * needs please refer to http://www.magentocommerce.com for more
   information.
 *
 * @category    design_default
 * @package     Mage
 * @copyright   Copyright (c) 2008 Irubin Consulting Inc. DBA Varien
   (http://www.varien.com)
 * @license     http://opensource.org/licenses/afl-3.0.php   Academic
   Free License (AFL 3.0)
 */
?>
<div class="box">
  <img src="<?php echo $this->
    getSkinUrl('images/media/col_right_callout.jpg') ?>"
    width="195"
    alt="<?php echo __('Keep your eyes open for our special Back to
    School items and save A LOT!') ?>" style="display:block;" />
</div>
```

 Note that the comments displayed at the top of this file are contained within < ?php> tags, which mean that the comments are not inserted in to our store's XHTML.

We need to change two values in the code of our new callout banner. They are the location of the callout graphic that we want to use, and the `alt` attribute of the image.

```
<div class="box">
  <img src="<?php echo
    $this->getSkinUrl('images/media/col_right_callout.jpg') ?>"
    width="195"
    alt="<?php echo __('Keep your eyes open for our special Back to
    School items and save A LOT!') ?>" style="display:block;" />
</div>
```

In our new `col_right.phtml` file in the `app/design/frontend/default/christmas/template/callouts/` directory, we'll change the name of the image to be used to our new callout graphic's filename `col_right_christmas.jpg`. We will also change the value of the `alt` text to a more relevant message (For example, `Christmas delivery discounts`):

```
<div class="box">
<img src="<?php echo $this->getSkinUrl('images/media/col_right_
christmas.jpg') ?>" width="195" alt="<?php echo __(Christmas delivery
discounts') ?>" style="display:block;" />
</div>
```

 If you're advertising discounts on delivery, don't forget to make sure you honor the discount. All you have to do is simply configure Magento to apply the discount for you!

In your Magento store's administration panel, under **Settings**, **Configuration**, **Design**, you'll need to set the **Skin (Images/CSS)** and **Templates** value, under the relevant scope (usually **Default Config**) to christmas:

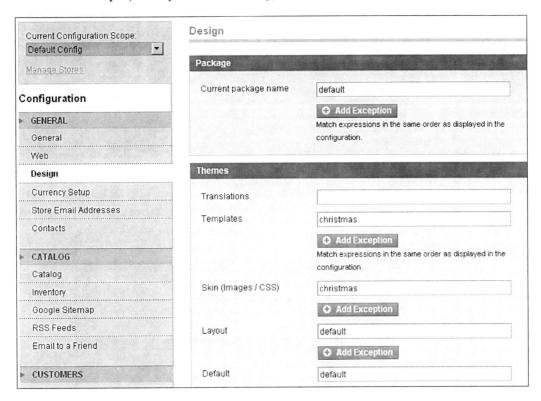

The new callout graphic is now displayed on our store, on the righthand column:

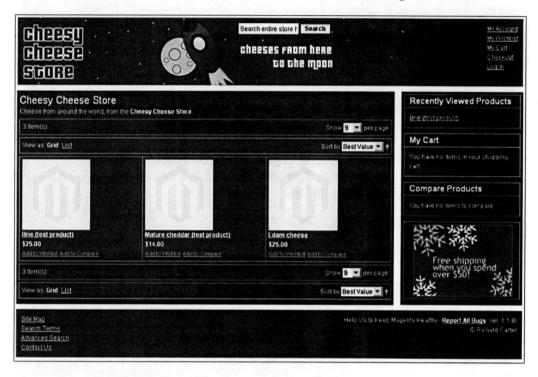

When the callout is no longer needed, you can revert to the settings that use the non-default theme:

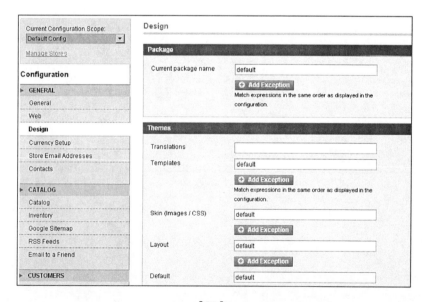

Summary

This chapter has focused on creating and using non-default themes with our Magento store. Along with looking at some uses for non-default themes, and the hierarchy of themes within Magento, we've looked at:

- How default and non-default themes affect your store
- Changing your store's header image with a non-default theme
- Changing your store's template files with a non-default theme
- Setting a non-default theme to display to your visitors

6
Advanced Magento Themes

As we've seen, we can change a lot of our Magento store by creating a Magento theme based upon an existing theme. We can take this further by looking at the following in more detail:

- Preparing the design for our new Magento theme
- Creating the layout, which our new Magento theme will need
- Creating the relevant blocks and templates for our store

Introducing our new design

A great way to understand clearly how Magento themes work is by customizing a theme more heavily than simply changing its logo or colors, which is what we'll do for our new Cheesy Cheese Store's design:

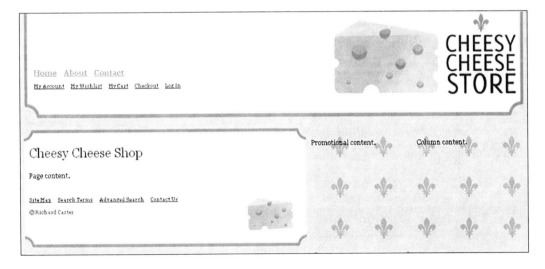

You'll notice that it's a three-column design, with a column for the primary information of the page, a column for promotional graphics (such as "free delivery this week"), and a last column for the shopping cart and other store-based functionality.

The design is achieved through some relatively simple XHMTL and CSS and a small number of images. The basic structure of our new theme contains:

- A header that contains the logo, navigation, and links to our visitors' accounts

- A left column, for the page's primary content

- A central column, for promotional graphics and messages for our store's visitors

- A righthand column, for our store's functionality such as shopping cart and product comparison feature

- A footer that contains our store's copyright notice and links to other store-wide features such as the **Site Map** and the **Advanced Search** feature. This is contained at the bottom of the lefthand column in our new Magento theme.

Magento is a huge system to work with. The easiest way to make sure that you don't miss anything while theming it is to simply install Magento's Blank theme again, and start from there. To distinguish it from our previous Magento theme, we will call our new skin `cheese2`, so copy the files from a clean copy of this theme in the `blank` directory in to a new directory called `cheese2`.

Creating skeleton templates

The next step in creating our new Magento theme is to create skeleton templates for our design. **Skeleton templates** provide the overall page structure for our Magento themes.

For example, we might want three different views in our store:

- Three columns, as shown in the previous screenshot

- Two columns with a column to the right

- Two columns with a column to the left

 Some Magento "themers" may find it easier to design their theme and create a static XHTML/CSS version of it before getting to this stage.

These three different options for your store would be achieved by creating three separate skeleton templates, and changing which of these templates is assigned to each module or page within our store using layout. We will use our three-column design throughout our new theme to ensure simplicity while we create our Magento theme. Our theme's skeleton template will look like this:

```
<!DOCTYPE html PUBLIC "-//W3C//DTD XHTML 1.0 Strict//EN"
    "http://www.w3.org/TR/xhtml1/DTD/xhtml1-strict.dtd">
<html xmlns="http://www.w3.org/1999/xhtml" xml:lang="en" lang="en">
  <head>
    <?php echo $this->getChildHtml('head') ?>
  </head>
  <body>
    <div id="wrapper">
      <?=$this->getChildHtml('header')?>
    </div>
    <div id="main">
      <div id="content">
        <?=$this->getChildHtml('content')?>
        <div id="footer">
          <?=$this->getChildHtml('footer')?>
        </div><!--/footer-->
      </div><!--/content-->
      <div id="left">
        <?=$this->getChildHtml('left')?>
        </div><!--/promo-->
        <div id="right">
          <?=$this->getChildHtml('right')?>
        </div><!--/column-->
      </div><!--/main-->
      <?php echo $this->getChildHtml('before_body_end') ?>
    </div><!--/wrapper-->
    <?php echo $this->getAbsoluteFooter() ?>
  </body>
</html>
```

 before_body_end is content that can be defined in Magento's administration panel, under **Configuration** | **Design** (under the **General** heading), and can be useful for inserting JavaScript such as that used for analytics in to your store.

We'll now save this skeleton template as `default.pthml` in the `app/design/frontend/default/cheese2/template/page` directory of our Magento installation, where `default` is the name of the Magento interface we're using, and `cheese2` is the name of our new Magento theme.

 If this file already exists, then you will need to overwrite it, as it provides a default page template for our Magento theme.

getChildHtml

The `getChildHtml` method used above inserts the relevant structural blocks in to the page. The value passed as a parameter to the `getChildHtml` method is the way in which each structural block is identified in the Magento layout files. Take this as an example:

```
<?=$this->getChildHtml('footer')?>
```

The value `footer` is passed as the parameter for the `getChildHtml` method, which references the `footer.phtml` template block in the `app/design/frontend/default/cheese2 /template/page/html` directory.

Assigning the skeleton template

We need to assign our new skeleton template to our Magento theme. We'll do this by opening the `page.xml` layout file in the `app/design/frontend/default/cheese2/layout` directory of our Magento store's installation, and change the template value to `page/default.phtml`.

```
<layout version="0.1.0">
  <default>
    <block type="page/html" name="root" output="toHtml"
      template="page/default.phtml">
    <!—layout continues -->
```

When the skeleton template is complete, we can begin to create blocks to populate content within the skeleton template.

Blocks in Magento

As we've seen, there are two types of blocks in a Magento theme—structural blocks and content blocks. The next step to creating our new Magento theme is to break our XHTML template in to blocks for Magento to handle.

Finding block paths in existing themes

If you're looking at an existing Magento theme, then try turning **Template Path Hints on**, which you can do from the administration panel. In **System | Configuration**, select your store in the drop-down box to the top left. Then select the **Developer** tab to the left, and select Yes for Template Path Hints, and save the changes to see paths of various blocks in Magento beside the blocks themselves within the template.

Structural blocks

Structural blocks in Magento contain one or more content blocks and are used to position these content blocks within each of our store's pages. The structural blocks in our store's new theme can be broken down in to the following:

- **Header**
- **Content**
- **Footer**
- **Left column**
- **Right column**

In the following image, each of the structural blocks is highlighted:

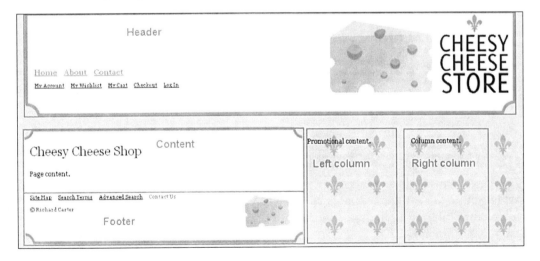

Content blocks

As you might expect, content blocks are the blocks that contain the content within each page in your Magento store. This type of block may include the following:

- **Store navigation**
- **Store access links**
- **Page content**
- **Footer content**
- **Callout**
- **Mini cart**
- **Newsletters**

In our new Cheesy Cheese Store design, we can pick out the elements in the following screenshot:

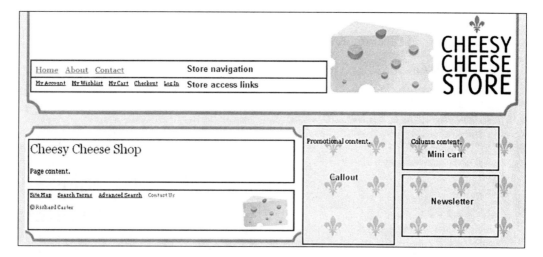

Inserting in to <head> tag

We'll start from the top of our original XHTML and work downwards. Therefore, the first template file is the one that is called within the `<head>` tag, called `head.phtml`, which you will find in the `app/design/frontend/default/cheese2/template/page/html` directory.

This content is not displayed within the page itself, but it is used (partially) to provide **metadata** about the page—information about the page itself, rather than any content of the page and to tell the search engines what the page is about.

```
<title><?php echo $this->getTitle() ?></title>
<meta http-equiv="Content-Type" content="
  <?php echo $this->getContentType() ?>" />
<meta name="description" content="
  <?php echo htmlspecialchars($this->getDescription()) ?>" />
<meta name="keywords" content="
  <?php echo htmlspecialchars($this->getKeywords()) ?>" />
<meta name="robots" content="
  <?php echo htmlspecialchars($this->getRobots()) ?>" />
<link rel="icon" href="<?php echo $this->
  getSkinUrl('favicon.ico') ?>" type="image/x-icon" />
<link rel="shortcut icon" href="<?php echo
  $this->getSkinUrl('favicon.ico') ?>" type="image/x-icon" />
<script type="text/javascript">
  //<![CDATA[
  var BLANK_URL = '<?php echo $this->
    helper('core/js')->getJsUrl('blank.html') ?>';
  var BLANK_IMG = '<?php echo $this->
    helper('core/js')->getJsUrl('spacer.gif') ?>';
  //]]>
</script>
<?php echo $this->getCssJsHtml() ?>
<?php echo $this->getChildHtml() ?>
<?php echo $this->helper('core/js')->getTranslatorScript() ?>
<?php echo $this->getIncludes() ?>
```

This template's code also ensures that Magento knows where to look for the CSS associated with our theme (as highlighted). Hence, we need not change any code.

Creating your store's header.phtml file

In our new store's design, `header.phtml` should contain the logo, navigation links, and what Magento calls the "store links", which include links to the customer's account on your store; such as to account features including their cart and a login (or logout) link. We need to open this file, in the `app/design/frontend/default/cheese2/templates/page/html` directory where Magento is installed, and make the following changes to it.

Store links

The `top.links.phtml` file inserts the code necessary for our Magento theme's "Store links".

```php
<?php if($toplinks && is_array($toplinks)): ?>
<ul class="shop-access">
  <?php echo $this->getChildHtml() ?>
  <?php foreach($toplinks as $_toplink): ?>
    <li<?php if($_toplink['first']||$_toplink['last']): ?>
      class="<?php if($_toplink['first']): ?>first
      <?php endif;?><?php if($_toplink['last']): ?>
      last <?php endif; ?>"<?php endif; ?>
      <?php echo $_toplink['liParams'] ?>>
    <?php echo $_toplink['beforeText'] ?>
    <a <?php echo $_toplink['aParams'] ?>>
    <?php echo $_toplink['innerText'] ?>
    </a><?php echo $_toplink['afterText'] ?></li>
  <?php endforeach; ?>
  </ul>
<?php endif; ?>
```

Although the PHP mentioned previously might look complicated, it generates the necessary links that your customers will need to access their account, depending on whether they are logged in to or out of your Magento store. This PHP creates an unordered list of these navigational items, which results in XHTML similar to the following code being generated, assuming you are not logged in to an account on the store:

```html
<ul class="shop-access">
  <li  class="first">
  <a href="https://yourstore.com/customer/account/"
    title="My Account" >My Account</a></li>
  <li ><a href="http://yourstore.com/wishlist/" title="My Wishlist"
    class="top-link-wishlist">My Wishlist</a></li>
  <li ><a href="http://yourstore.com/checkout/cart/"
    title="My Cart" class="top-link-cart">My Cart</a></li>
  <li ><a href="http://yourstore.com/checkout/"
    title="Checkout" class="top-link-checkout">Checkout</a></li>
  <li  class="last">
    <a href="https://yourstore.com/customer/account/login/"
      title="Log In" >Log In</a>
  </li>
</ul>
```

Note that the first and last list items are identified with a class (`.first` and `.last`). This may be useful if you need these links to be styled slightly differently than the other links in the list.

Altering your store's logo

You may recall that the logo in your Magento store can be changed through Magento's administration panel. To ensure that our new theme for Magento allows the logo and the `alt` text for the logo to be changed with Magento's control panel, we may need to make some changes to the code that refers to the store's logo within the `header.phtml` file:

```
<a href="#" title="<?php echo $this->getLogoAlt() ?>">
  <img id="logo" src="<?php echo $this->getLogoSrc() ?> "
    alt="<?php echo $this->getLogoAlt() ?>" />
</a>
```

`<?php echo $this->getLogoAlt() ?>` inserts the alternative (`alt`) text associated with the logo to the page, while `<?php echo $this->getLogoSrc() ?>` inserts the address of the logo set in the administration panel to the page. **You shouldn't need to change this code though.**

Finally, we need to save the logo file in the `skin/frontend/default/cheese2/images` directory.

Changing the logo using Magento's administration panel

This assumes that our store's **Logo Image Src** value is set to **images/logo.gif** in the administration panel. If we want to use a logo with a different filename, then we can simply edit these values, which can be found under the **System | Configuration** options within the **Design** tab, and then upload the new logo to the images directory.

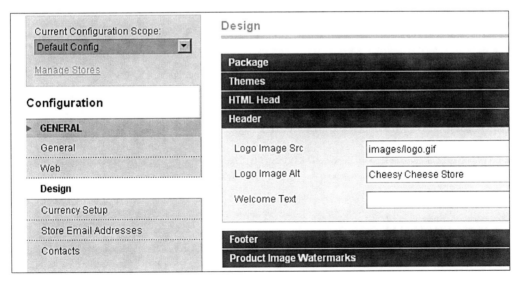

Our `header.phtml` file is now complete.

Footer.phtml

The footer contains links to the store's advanced search feature, site map, and RSS feeds. Our `footer.phtml` file is quite short, and it contains the following code:

```
<div class="informational">
  <?php echo $this->getChildHtml() ?>
</div>
<p class="legality">
  <?php echo $this->getCopyright() ?>
</p>
```

This gives us content, similar to the following in the footer of our page:

```
<div class="informational">
  <ul>
    <li  class="first">
      <a href="http://yourstore.com/catalog/seo_sitemap/category/"
        title="Site Map" >Site Map</a></li>
    <li >
      <a href="http://yourstore.com/catalogsearch/term/popular/"
        title="Search Terms" >Search Terms</a></li>
    <li >
      <a href="http://yourstore.com/catalogsearch/advanced/"
        title="Advanced Search" >Advanced Search</a></li>
    <li >
      <a href="http://yourstore.com/contacts/"
        title="Contact Us" >Contact Us</a></li>
    <li  class="last">
      <a href="http://yourstore.com/rss/"
        title="RSS testing" class="link-feed">RSS</a></li>
  </ul>
</div>
<p class="legality">
  &copy; Richard Carter
</p>
```

Luckily, there's nothing we need to change in the `footer.phtml` template for our theme, so we can leave it as it appeared within Magento's Blank theme.

Pager.phtml

The `pager.phtml` file creates the necessary code for pagination, when required. The code is as it appears in the original theme, so we need not change this as well.

Wrapper.phtml

Lastly, for our page templates, we can create `wrapper.phtml`. While this file is not used within most views of your Magento store, it's useful to leave it as it appears in Magento's default theme. This is because certain views within Magento make use of it (like the AJAX loader).

```php
<?php $_tag = $this->hasTag() ? $this->getTag() : "div" ?>
<<?php echo $_tag?> id="<?php echo $this->getId()?>"
   <?php echo $this->getParams()?>>
<?php echo $this->getChildHtml()?>
   </<?php echo $_tag?>>
```

Magento's IDs and classes

When creating themes that you intend to share with other Magento users, it can be helpful to use the same naming conventions used in Magento's default themes for the elements you use in your store. They can also be a useful reference while creating CSS for your Magento theme.

CSS ID/class	Description
`.wrapper`	This usually contains all of the store's content within the `<body>` element and can be used to center the design, if necessary.
`#logo`	This ID refers to the store's logo, usually contained within an `<h1>` element.
`.header`	It is usual for the store's logo, search feature, and customer links to be contained within the header, though the beauty of theming Magento is that you can change these if you desire!
`.shop-access`	The shop access element is used to contain links to Magento's customer features such as customer accounts, carts, and wishlist.
`.header-nav`	The header navigation class is used to contain your store's navigation links. These often consist of categories and sub-categories of your store.
`.breadcrumbs`	The `breadcrumbs` class is used to contain the "breadcrumbs" of links that help to orientate your store's customers as to where they are in your store.
`.head`	This class is used to contain heading elements (for example, the `<h1>` element) in the main body. Depending on your theme's design, you may find that these are unnecessary.
`.content`	The content class is used to wrap content within the store.
`.legality`	The legality class is usually applied to the copyright notice in the footer of your Magento store, which can be edited through Magento's CMS.

As Magento is a powerful e-commerce system, there are a huge number of these IDs and classes to consider, and listing them all here would be overwhelming. If you are curious, then the easiest way to find them is to check the source HTML of your page and locate the area you are interested in.

Styling with CSS

We can now style our theme's XHTML structure with some CSS. Remember that a Magento theme's CSS file is stored in the `skin/frontend/default/cheese2/css` directory, where `cheese2` is the name of your theme.

Reset CSS

Firstly, we'll use some reset CSS to make sure that the browser's default values don't affect our new Magento theme.

```css
address, caption, cite, code, dfn, th{
  font-style:normal;
  font-weight:normal
}
abbr, acronym{
  border:0
}
body, html{
  margin:0;
  padding:0
}
blockquote, body, div, dl, dt, dd, fieldset, form, h1, h2, h3, h4, h5,
h6, input, li, ol, ul, p, pre, textarea, td, th{
  margin:0; padding:0
}
  caption, th{
  text-align:left
}
h1, h2, h3, h4, h5, h6, p, pre, blockquote{
  background:transparent;
  font-weight:normal;
  word-spacing:0px
}
fieldset, img{
  border:0
}
table{
  border-collapse:collapse;
  border-spacing:0
}
```

Secondly, we'll add some generic styling to elements such as links, headings, and the <body>, giving a general style in terms of colors and typography. The font-size of the body is set to 62.5%, which helps to make the text size more stable across browsers.

```
body {
  background: #F7F4E7 url("images/body_bg.png") repeat top left;
  color: #000;
  font-family: "georgia", "times new roman", "times", serif;
  font-size: 62.5%
}
h1, h2, h3, h4, h5, h6 {font-weight: bold;line-height: 200%}
h1 {color: #333}
h2 {color: #C6AD52;font-size: 100%;line-height: 125%}
h3 {line-height: 110%;text-transform: uppercase}
h4, h5, h6 {color: #C6AD52;font-size: 100%;line-height: 100%}
a, a:link, a:active {color: #333}
a:hover {color: #09C;text-decoration: none}
.no-display {display: none !important}
```

Note that we define the .no-display class, and apply the CSS display: none to it, as this is another CSS class that many Magento themes make use of.

We'll now add more specific styles to the remaining elements on our page by styling .wrapper that surrounds the store's content to be centralized within the browser window. We'll also add style to get the logo to display where it is needed—to the top right of the screen.

```
.wrapper {
  margin: 0 auto;
  width: 950px
}
img#logo {
  /* NB: we're not using a h1 for the logo */
  display: inline;
  float:right;
  margin-bottom: 10px;
  padding: 0 10px 0 0
}
.header {
  background: transparent url("images/header_bg.png")
    no-repeat top    right;
  height: 193px;
  margin-bottom: 20px
}
```

Next, we'll style the store's navigation and "shop access" links, which appear in the new theme's header area.

```css
ul#nav {
   float: left;font-size: 135%;
   list-style-type: none;
   padding: 100px 0 0 20px
}
#nav li {display: inline;margin-right: 10px}
#nav a {color: #C6AD52;font-weight: bold}
#nav a:hover, .shop-access a:hover {color: #09C}
ul.shop-access {
   background: #FFF;
   clear: left;
   list-style-type: none;
   margin: 10px 0 10px 20px !important;
   padding: 10px 0;
   width: 500px
}
.shop-access li {display: inline;margin-right: 10px}
.shop-access a {color: #333}
```

The content areas are the next to be styled. We'll apply widths to each of the three columns in the content area of our store, and apply `float: left` to them to achieve our three-column layout.

 Where a `float` is declared, we also apply `display: inline`, which overcomes problems in certain versions of Internet Explorer.

```css
#main {
   clear: both;
   font-size: 120%
}
#main a {
   color: #09C
}
#main p, #main ul, #main ol, #main dl {
   margin: 10px 0
}
#main ol, #main ul {
   margin-left: 15px
}
#main img {
   clear: right;
   float: right;
   margin: 10px 0 10px 10px
}
```

```
#main img.float_left {
  clear: left !important;margin: 10px 10px 0 0 !important
}
#content a:visited {
  color: #666
}
#content, #left, #right {
  display: inline;
  float: left
}
p.contact {
  border-top: 1px #666 dotted;
  border-bottom: 1px #666 dotted;
  color: #666;
  font-size: 110%;
  padding: 5px 0
}
.contact span {
  font-weight: bold
}
#content {
  background: #FFF url("images/content_bg.png") no-repeat top left;
  padding: 20px 10px 0 10px;
  width: 515px
}
#left, #right {
  padding: 10px;
  width: 180px
}
#left h2 {
  text-align: center
}
```

Lastly, we'll style the footer, while making sure to display the background image.

```
#footer {
  background: #FFF url("images/footer_bg.png") no-repeat bottom left;
  clear: both;
  color: #666;
  font-size: 80%;
  height: 75px;
  margin: 0 -10px !important;
  padding: 20px 150px 20px 10px;
  width: 375px
}
#footer ul {
  list-style-type: none;
  margin: 0
}
#footer li {
```

```
  display: inline;
  margin-right: 10px
}
#footer a {
  color: #333
}
#footer a:hover {
  color: #09C
}
```

Organize your CSS!

Notice that it's easier to find what you're looking for in your CSS file if the attributes (such as background, color, margin, padding, and so on) are organized alphabetically. You'll especially notice the effects of this in larger CSS files.

Before seeing the changes, you will need to have turned Magento's cache off!

Turning the cache off

In order to make testing and perfecting our new Magento theme easier, we can turn the cache off under the **System | Cache Management** option of your Magento store's administration panel:

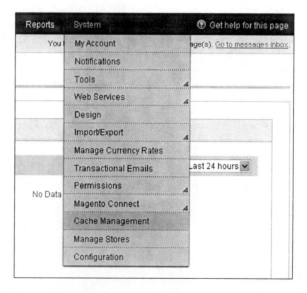

From there, simply select the **Disable** option from the drop-down list:

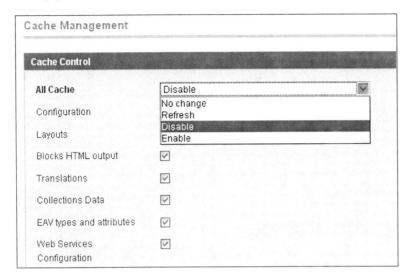

Save this setting, and the system cache will be disabled.

 Don't forget to turn the system cache **On** when your store launches—it will help reduce load on your store's server!

Refresh the page in your browser, and we will see a design similar to the following screenshot, assuming the relevant images are in the correct directory.

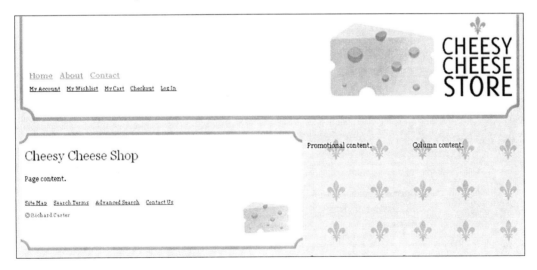

Creating a favicon

Our Magento skin can also include a favicon file as well. All we need to do is save a
`favicon.ico` file in the skin directory of our theme. In the case of the Cheesy Cheese
Store's new theme, we'd save our favicon as `skin/frontend/default/cheese2/`
`favicon.ico`.

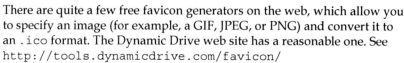

Favicon generators

There are quite a few free favicon generators on the web, which allow you
to specify an image (for example, a GIF, JPEG, or PNG) and convert it to
an `.ico` format. The Dynamic Drive web site has a reasonable one. See
`http://tools.dynamicdrive.com/favicon/`

Setting the theme

As always, we need to set our new Magento theme in the administration panel, from
the **Configuration** section located under the **System** tab in the navigation. In the
Design tab to the left, you can change the values of **Templates**, **Skins**, and **Layout**
under the **Themes** heading to the name of our new theme – `cheese2`.

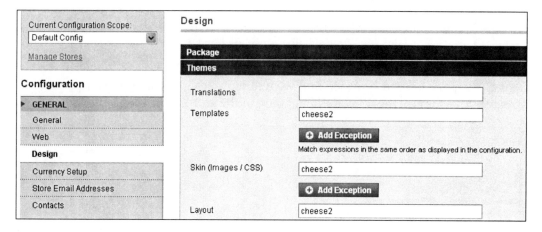

After saving these settings, we should be able to see any changes we make to our
new theme.

Remember to disable Magento's cache in your store's administration
panel. Without doing this, you will not be able to see the changes to
your theme.

Summary

In this chapter, we began to look at creating more complex Magento themes, while going through the following:

- Creating a skeleton template for our theme
- Turning that HTML in to the blocks that Magento requires
- Starting our theme's layout files
- Creating the skin for our theme

Next, we'll look at completing our theme's template files and layout files.

7
Further Magento Theming

In the previous chapter, we began to create our store's new Magento theme from an XHTML and CSS template. There are still template and layout files in our Magento theme that we can change. We'll complete our new Magento theme in this chapter, while editing the template and layout files again, as well as making some changes to the skin.

If you have not done so already, then make sure that all of the files from a clean copy of Magento's Blank theme reside in the relevant directories for our `cheese2` theme.

The layout and template files are in the `app/design/frontend/default/cheese2` directory. Template files can be found in the `template` subdirectory, while layout files should reside in the `layout` subdirectory. The skin files—CSS, images, and JavaScript need to be in the `skin/frontend/default/cheese2` directory.

Theming tasks

The easiest way to get a grip on Magento theming is to undertake some tasks to change your theme. What you learn from these tasks can be applied to similar situations in other areas of theming your Magento store. To this end, we'll look at the following:

- Customizing our theme's product page
- Customizing navigation in our store
- Creating a custom "page not found" error page
- Using a layout to adapt our Magento theme further

After looking at how these changes are achieved using Magento's layout and template files, you'll have a better understanding of how Magento themes and their files work together to produce what you see on the screen.

Customizing the product page

First and perhaps the most obvious task that we can undertake is to change our theme's product page. At the moment, the default content area looks like the following image:

Product pages currently look like this without any styling applied to their various elements:

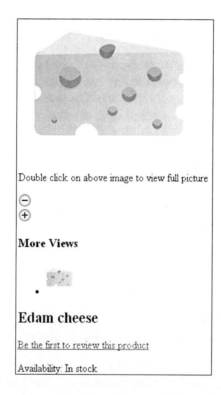

With basic styling inherited from the Blank theme's `styles.css` file (located in `skin/frontend/default/cheese2/css` directory), our product page looks much more presentable:

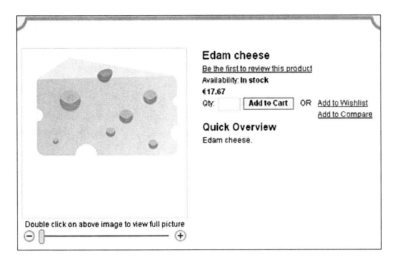

We can continue to edit the CSS attributes, which are related to how products are displayed to our desire. Great improvements to your store's look and feel can be made simply by manipulating the CSS provided in the Blank theme to suit your store's color scheme. This can be incredibly time-consuming for Magento theme designers.

Improving content hierarchy for better search engine results

The product view page template for our theme is located in the `app/design/frontend/default/cheese2/template/catalog/product` directory, and is called `view.phtml`. Our primary motivation behind editing this template is to improve the hierarchy of the content within our store's product page, which can lead to improved search engine results for your store's products.

Within `view.phtml`, locate the following snippet of code, which inserts the short description for the product:

```
<h4><?php echo $this->__('Quick Overview') ?></h4>
<div class="short-description">
  <?php echo $_helper->productAttribute($_product,
  nl2br($_product->getShortDescription()), 'short_description') ?>
</div>
```

By adding the name of the product into the <h4> heading element (for which the code is highlighted below), we can instantly make it obvious about what the Quick Overview relates to:

```
<h4>
  <?php echo $this->__('Quick Overview for ') ?>
  <?php echo $_helper->productAttribute($_product,
    $this->htmlEscape($_product->getName()), 'name') ?>
</h4>
<div class="short-description">
  <?php echo $_helper->productAttribute($_product,
    nl2br($_product->getShortDescription()), 'short_description') ?>
</div>
```

Not only does this change group related information together in a more logical way, but it also helps to give search engines crawling your Magento store a better idea of what the purpose of the page is, helping you to attract customers looking for products sold on your store.

 Experiment with what works best for your store's design and layout, by making use of Magento's non-default theme feature.

Customizing Magento's navigation

Navigation is an important element of your Magento store, allowing your customers to find what they're looking for more easily. In some circumstances, your store's navigation may not be displayed in your theme, which we can address now.

Displaying Navigation in Magento

If your store's navigation isn't displayed yet, log in to your store's administration panel and ensure each category that you want to show in the navigation is a sub-category of the root category.

By default, this root category is called **Default Category**. Make sure that the **IsActive** setting on this root category is set to **Yes**.

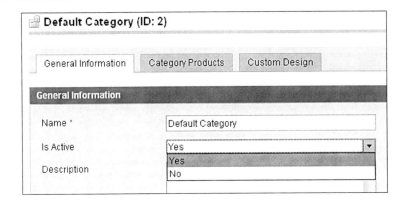

Select the category from the **Catalog | Manage Categories** option in the administration panel to set the root category as the parent of another category in your store.

Creating a new root category

If your store does not have a root category, then you'll need to create one to assign your other categories to, or else your store's navigation won't be displayed. To create a new root category, you select the **Add Root Category** option within the **Catalog | Manage Categories** in your administration panel.

Once you have completed the fields, you'll be able to add categories beneath this root category, which can then be displayed in the theme's navigation.

Editing the navigation

If you want to edit your store's navigation, then you can find the template file called `top.phtml` in the `app/design/frontend/default/cheese2/template/catalog/navigation` directory of your Magento store's installation by adding CSS to our theme's `styles.css` file in the `skin/frontend/default/cheese2/css` directory.

Styling the navigation

The CSS we've added has already styled the navigation, and after refreshing the page we should see some of our store's product categories appear, as shown in the following image:

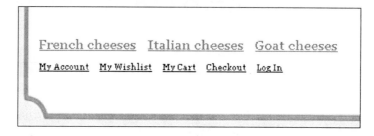

We can also customize how our store's navigation looks further by editing the `skin/frontend/default/cheese2/css/styles.css` file.

Creating a custom "not found" page

You can easily create your own "not found" error page to be displayed when a customer encounters a `404` error on your store. In your store's administration panel, select **Manage Pages** from under the **CMS** option, and for the **SEF URL Identifier** field, be sure to enter a value of **no-route**, which tells Magento that the page is to be used as your custom "not found" error page:

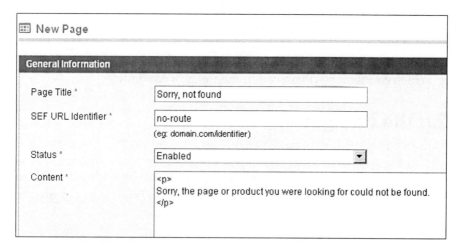

Before saving the page, ensure that the **Status** is set to **Enabled**: your custom `404` error page is complete!

Creating a "not found" page using templates

An alternative error page for your Magento store can be created using your theme's templates. This can be done using the `no-route.phtml` template in the `app/design/frontend/default/cheese2/template/cms/default` directory. This template is displayed if no `404` (not found) page exists in the Magento CMS.

Advanced layouts in Magento

Layouts for our new theme are stored in the `app/design/frontend/default/cheese2/layout` directory. While editing templates allows changes to our theme's functionality and appearance on a smaller basis, changing a theme's layout files can have a wider effect upon your store's appearance. Magento recognizes two types of layouts:

- Default layouts
- Layout updates

Default layouts

A default layout does exactly what you would expect it to—it provides the layout that is used by default in Magento. That is, unless you specify a page or module-specific layout for any particular view within your store, the default layout will be used.

Layout updates

Layout updates are used by Magento to update the layout from its default to an alternative layout. Layout updates can also be used to specify CSS or JavaScript files that you no longer need loaded for each page.

```
<!-- omitted layout -->
<reference name="root">
  <action method="setTemplate">
    <template>page/update-layout-template.phtml</template>
  </action>
</reference>
<!-- omitted layout -->
```

It's the `<action>` element that allows the template to be referenced and the page's layout to be updated.

 The `<action>` element can be used in Magento's default layouts too.

With all of the style for our new theme in one CSS file, `styles.css`, in the `skin/frontend/default/cheese2/css` directory, we no longer need to reference other CSS files that form part of the default Magento theme.

How Magento layouts work

The Magento layouts allow great flexibility in themes through a small number of XML elements.

Handles in layout

The layout handles help Magento to determine where to apply the instructions within it. There are two primary types of handles in Magento—default and non-default. If a handle is set as `<default>`, then the layout within the handle is applied to the page before any page-specific layout instruction.

If the handle is not `<default>`, then the layout is imposed upon the relevant page. For example, if the handle is `<sendfriend_product_send>` in `sendfriend.xml`, the layout update applies only to the *send to a friend* form feature.

Layout blocks

If you remember, there are two types of blocks in Magento—structural blocks and content blocks, which can now be distinguished in the layout files. In the layout files, the structural blocks contain the `as` attribute, and assign the relevant Magento templates to the right area of the skeleton template within our theme. The `<block>` element has a number of attributes that can be used within it, including:

- `action`
- `after` and `before`
- `as`
- `name`
- `type`

The action attribute

The `action` attribute is used to load skin files such as JavaScript and CSS in to the `<head>` element of your Magento store. For example, the following code would load the JavaScript file `jquery.min.js` in the `jquery` directory of your theme's skin directory:

```
<action method="addJs">
<script>jquery/jquery.min.js</script>
</action>
```

The as attribute

The `as` attribute in a Magento layout is the name assigned to a block by a template. For example, where you see `<block as "header">` within a layout file, the block known as `header` in your theme's skeleton template is what it references.

The after and before attributes

The `after` and `before` attributes are used to specify whether a block within layout should appear after or before a structural block, respectively.

The type attribute

The `type` attribute identifies the module such as Catalog Search or the Newsletter module, which the layout refers to. It defines what the block does, so if you're unfamiliar with this, it's best to leave it as it appears within the layout files.

Layout references

Magento layout files also make use of `<reference>` elements, which are used to make references to another block. In contrast with the `type` attribute, the reference element in a Magento layout affects the page layout on a small basis, allowing blocks from within modules (like the mini-cart feature of the shopping cart module) to be placed within other modules of your store.

addJS in layout

References to JavaScript files can be added using the `addJS` action. The references are given relative to the path of your Magento installation. The following code from the layout above adds the `effects.js` file located in the `scriptaculous` directory of our Magento store's installation:

```
<action method="addJs">
  <script>scriptaculous/effects.js</script>
</action>
```

addCss in layout

The `addCss` action in a Magento layout file ensures that a CSS file is loaded in to the `<head>` element of your store. The following layout instruction, taken from the previous code snippet, adds a CSS file named `style.css` in the `skin/frontend/default/cheese2/css` directory, where `cheese2` is the name of the current Magento theme.

```
<action method="addCss">
  <stylesheet>css/style.css</stylesheet>
</action>
```

This method allows specific CSS files to be loaded in to the page for particular features, if necessary.

as in layout

The as attribute allows Magento to know which areas of the skeleton template(s) to replace with which templates. The layout code below tells Magento that the header.phtml file in the theme's template directory is to be inserted wherever getChildHtml('header') is found in our skeleton template.

```
<block type="page/html_header" name="header" as="header">
```

When we were creating the skeleton template for our theme, we kept references to the content blocks consistent, calling them content, right, and left. Although we can change these values by making use of the as attribute, it's much easier to keep them consistent with other Magento themes, as it will help to prevent a lot of changes being needed in our theme's layout files.

Removing a layout

As well as adding information to specific pages with a layout, Magento allows you to remove references to blocks and other information, which a layout doesn't require.

For example, take this layout from catalogsearch.xml in the app/design/frontend/default/cheese2/layout directory, which references the 1column.phtml skeleton template:

```
<catalogsearch_term_popular>
  <remove name="right"/>
  <remove name="left"/>
  <reference name="root">
    <action method="setTemplate">
      <template>page/1column.phtml</template>
    </action>
  </reference>
  <reference name="content">
  <block type="catalogsearch/term" name="seo.searchterm"
    template="catalogsearch/term.phtml"/>
  </reference>
</catalogsearch_term_popular>
```

Here, we can delete the <remove> elements from the XML so that the right and left columns appear in our page for the list of most popular search terms used on our store. The final layout for this block looks like this:

```
<catalogsearch_term_popular>
  <reference name="content">
    <block type="catalogsearch/term" name="seo.searchterm"
      template="catalogsearch/term.phtml"/>
  </reference>
</catalogsearch_term_popular>
```

> **Don't see any changes?**
> If the changes to your layout files don't seem to be working, then
> check if every element is either self-closed or closed by a matching
> close tag, and be sure that your store's cache is disabled.

Summary

The templates and layout needed for our new default Magento theme are now
complete. In this chapter, we've:

- Manipulated our theme's templates
- Added the remaining images and CSS for our theme's skin
- Edited layout files to make changes to our theme where needed

We're closer to completing our Magento theme now; our theme is fully functioning
as an online store.

There are still some things you may wish to change to improve upon your store's
new theme, but you should now have the skill to know what to change and how to
make the change. We'll move on to improving our Magento store by adding a social
aspect to it and providing a good print style.

8
Social Media in Magento

Our theming of Magento does not have to stop at changing the way it looks. We can also add aspects of social media to it, such as:

- Integrating your Magento store with Twitter
- Improving your store's customer service
- Using social bookmarking tools such as AddThis to help your customers spread the word about your store across the Internet

With so many e-commerce stores on the Internet, using social media can make a huge difference to your store's fortunes. It can also increase your potential customers and ensure that customers continue to come back.

Integrating Twitter with Magento

Twitter (http://twitter.com) is a micro-blogging service, which allows its users to send short messages to their followers, answering the question "what are you doing now?"

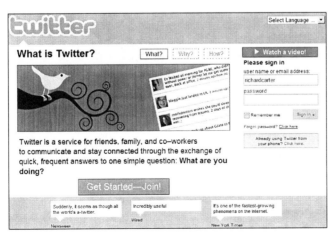

After registering a Twitter account, you can begin to *follow* other Twitter users. When they update their status, you will see it in your *timeline* of what people you follow say.

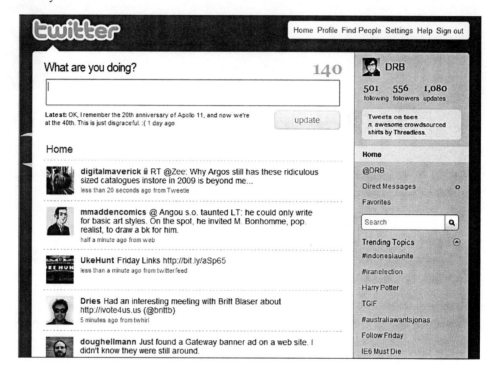

 When you sign up for a Twitter account, it is usually best to sign up as the name of your store—for example, "Cheesy Cheese Store" rather than "RichardCarter", simply because your customers are more likely to search for the name of the store rather than your own name.

Tweeting: Ideas for your store's tweets

If you look at other businesses on Twitter, you'll see that there are a number of ways to promote your store on Twitter without losing followers by being too "spammy".

- Some companies give voucher codes to Twitter followers—a good way to entice new customers
- Others use Twitter to host competitions for free items—a good way to reward existing customers
- You can also release products to your Twitter followers before releasing them to other customers

Displaying your Twitter updates on your Magento store

Twitter can be a powerful tool for your store on its own, but you can integrate Twitter with your Magento store to drive existing customers to your Twitter account, which can help to generate repeat customers.

There are a few ways Twitter can be used with Magento, the most versatile of which is the LazzyMonks Twitter module.

Installing the LazzyMonks Twitter module

To install the LazzyMonks module, visit its page on the Magento Commerce web site (`http://www.magentocommerce.com/extension/482/lazzymonks-twitter`), and retrieve the extension key, after agreeing to the terms and conditions. Log in to your Magento store's administration panel, and open the **Magento Connect Manager** in the **Magento Connect** option under the **System** tab.

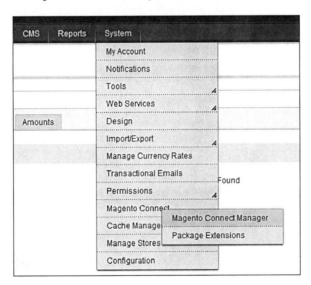

Once this has loaded, paste the extension key in to the text box next to the **Paste extension key to install** label, as shown in the following screenshot:

This will install the module for you. Return to your Magento store's administration panel, and you will see a Twitter option in the navigation. The **View Tweets** option allows you to view updates made to your Twitter account. The **Post Update** option allows you to update Twitter from your store's administration panel.

Firstly, you will need to configure the module's settings, which can be found under the **Twitter** option of the **Configuration** section of your store's administration panel, under the **System** tab.

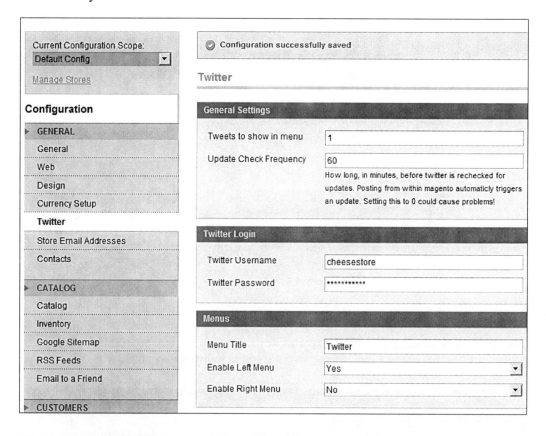

The **Twitter Login** options are of particular interest. Here you will need to enter your Twitter account's username and password.

Once this has been saved, you can post a status update to your Twitter account through Magento's administration panel:

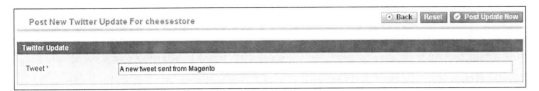

This then appears on your Twitter account:

Your tweets will also be displayed on your store, as a block beneath other content and can be styled with CSS in your Magento theme by addressing div.twitter.

Other ways to integrate Twitter with Magento

The other way to integrate your Twitter feed with Magento is by embedding Twitter's widgets into your site. To use these, log in to your Twitter account, and go to http://twitter.com/widgets. You can then use the HTML provided within the Magento templates to insert your Twitter updates into your store.

Adding your Twitter feed through Magento's CMS

Alternatively, you can insert your Twitter account's updates into any page managed through Magento's Content Management System. In Magento's administration panel, select **CMS | Manage Pages**, and select the page that you want your Twitter stream to appear in. Within your page, simply paste the code that Twitter produces when you select the type of Twitter "badge", which you want to display on your store.

 Consider creating a new block for your Twitter statuses, so that it can be removed from pages where it is likely to be distracting (for example, the checkout page).

Integrating Get Satisfaction with Magento

Get Satisfaction (http://getsatisfaction.com) is an "unofficial" customer support service. There are other similar customer satisfaction services such as eKomi (http://www.ekomi.co.uk), which can be integrated with Magento in a similar fashion.

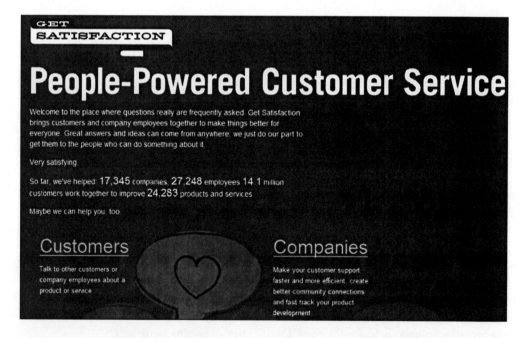

Though there are currently no modules for Magento, you may want to consider signing up for a **Get Satisfaction** account and adding a link to your store's footer area, asking for customer feedback. Free accounts are available, although the number of visits per month your account can receive is limited.

By resolving problems and answering questions in an open way, you can actively enhance your store's reputation online, so expect what seem to be silly or pointless questions (they could help you to improve your store's design in the future) and remain polite and friendly!

To add the link, sign up for a company account on **Get Satisfaction**. Open your store's administration panel, and select the **Static blocks** option under **CMS**:

You can now select the **Footer links** static block from the list:

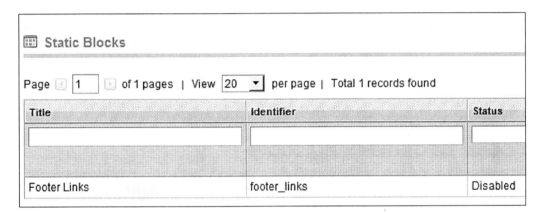

The address of the Cheesy Cheese Store's **Get Satisfaction** account is `http://www.getsatisfaction.com/cheesycheesestore`, so we need to add a link to this in the content.

By default, the content already in the **Footer Links** block is similar to:

```
<ul>
    <li><a href="{{store url=""}}about">About Us</a></li>
    <li class="last"><a href="{{store url=""}}
      customer-service">Customer Service</a></li>
</ul>
```

We'll change the **Customer service** link currently there to **Customer feedback**, and link to our store's **Get Satisfaction** account.

```
<ul>
  <li>
    <a href="{{store url=""}}about-magento-demo-store">About Us</a>
  </li>
  <li class="last">
    <a href="http://www.getsatisfaction.com/cheesycheesestore"
      title="Customer feedback">Customer feedback</a>
  </li>
</ul>
```

Once you have saved these changes, the new link will appear in your store's footer.

Integrating social bookmarking with Magento

Social bookmarking services allow users to store and organize links to their favorite web sites online. By integrating social bookmarking with your Magento store, you allow customers to interact with your business outside the confines of your store, ensuring that your customers are still considering your products elsewhere.

Social bookmarking tools

There are a huge number of these services on the web, but some bookmarking tools are more popular than others. The following are a few examples:

- Digg (`http://digg.com`)
- Delicious (`http://delicious.com`)
- Mister Wong (`http://www.mister-wong.com`), which is particularly popular in Germany
- Facebook (`http://www.facebook.com`)

Your store's web pages could become very crowded if you listed every service available. Luckily, there are services that allow your visitors to choose which service to save their link to, for example:

- AddThis
- Socializer

These allow much easier integration with social bookmarking tools, as they aggregate at least the most popular services into one.

Socializer

Ekstreme's Socializer (`http://ekstreme.com/socializer`) allows users to bookmark a huge range of bookmarking services. Creating a link to Socializer is simple. You pass an address (URL) and the title of the page to be bookmarked. A link to Socializer looks like this:

```
<a
   href='http://ekstreme.com/socializer/?
      url=http://www.yourstore.com&title=Title+of+your+store'
      title='Bookmark this page'>Bookmark this page>
</a>
```

Your visitor is then presented with a page similar to the following screenshot, with options to save the page in various bookmarking services:

AddThis

AddThis (`http://www.addthis.com`) **is the #1 bookmarking and sharing service,** allowing visitors to your store to bookmark your Magento store with over 50 different online bookmarking services.

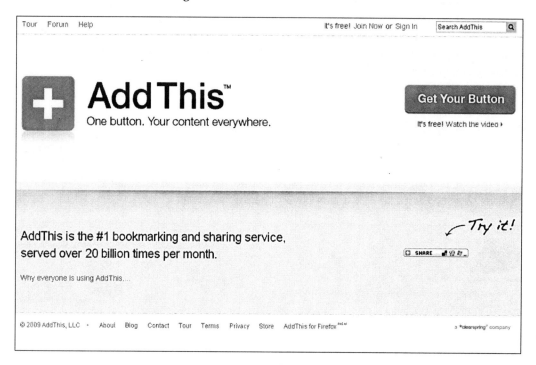

AddThis also allows its users to save the page to their preferred bookmarking service. It also has options for the user to print the page and email a friend too.

You can use **AddThis** without registering, but registering allows you to track which pages are being shared and how.

Using AddThis in Magento

As **AddThis** offers more options to our visitors, we'll use it in the Cheesy Cheese Store's new theme. The first step to using **AddThis** in Magento is to select which button you would like to display. Go to http://www.addthis.com/web-button-select, and make a selection. For Cheesy Cheese Store, we'll use the option that we saw previously. The code that **AddThis** generates looks like this:

```
<!-- AddThis Button BEGIN -->
  <script type="text/javascript">
    var addthis_pub="4a0c2aff012daef5";
  </script>
  <a href="http://www.addthis.com/bookmark.php?v=20"
     onmouseover="return addthis_open(this, '', '[URL]',
     '[TITLE]')"onmouseout="addthis_close()" onclick="return
     addthis_sendto()">
    <img src="http://s7.addthis.com/static/btn/lg-bookmark-en.gif"
     width="125" height="16" alt="Bookmark and Share"
     style="border:0"/>
  </a>
  <script type="text/javascript"
     src="http://s7.addthis.com/js/200/addthis_widget.js"></script>
<!-- AddThis Button END -->
```

 When you sign up to **AddThis**, you'll be given your own publisher identity number, which you'll need to use to replace the publisher identity number shown in the previous code snippet.

We can add this to the addto.phtml template file in our Magento theme, which can be found in the app/design/frontend/default/cheese2/template/catalog/product/view directory.

```
<?php $_product = $this->getProduct() ?>
<ul class="add-to-box">
<?php if ($this->helper('wishlist')->isAllow()) : ?>
  <li>
    <a href="<?php echo $this->helper
    ('wishlist')->getAddUrl($_product)      ?>"><?php echo $this
    ->__('Add to Wishlist') ?></a>
  </li>
<?php endif; ?>
```

```php
<?php if($_compareUrl=$this->helper('catalog/product_compare')
  ->getAddUrl($_product) ): ?>
  <li>
    <span class="pipe">|</span> <a href="<?php echo $_compareUrl
      ?>"><?php echo $this->__('Add to Compare') ?></a>
  </li>
  <?php endif; ?>
</ul>
```

We can add our link just above the closing `</ul>`:

```html
<!-- AddThis Button BEGIN -->
<li><script type="text/javascript">var addthis_
pub="4a0c2aff012daef5";</script>
<a href="http://www.addthis.com/bookmark.php?v=20" onmouseover="return
addthis_open(this, '', '[URL]', '[TITLE]')" onmouseout="addthis_
close()" onclick="return addthis_sendto()"><img src="http://
s7.addthis.com/static/btn/lg-bookmark-en.gif" width="125" height="16"
alt="Bookmark and Share" style="border:0"/></a></li>
<script type="text/javascript" src="http://s7.addthis.com/js/200/
addthis_widget.js"></script>
<!-- AddThis Button END -->
```

This will mean that the AddThis button will be displayed alongside the links to compare products and to add a product to your Magento store. We can also remove the last `<script>` element from the code highlighted above, by using a Magento layout file to add it to the `<head>` of category pages.

To change the layout of our theme, we need to edit the `catalog.xml` file in the `app/design/frontend/default/cheese2/layout` directory. Locate the section (usually near the top) that looks like this:

```xml
<default>
  <reference name="top.menu">
    <block type="catalog/navigation" name="catalog.topnav"
      template="catalog/navigation/top.phtml"/>
  </reference>
```

We can insert a snippet of XML in to the relevant layout file so that Magento only inserts the JavaScript files required by AddThis when they are needed.

```xml
<default>
  <reference name="top.menu">
    <block type="catalog/navigation" name="catalog.topnav"
      template="catalog/navigation/top.phtml"/>
  </reference>
  <reference name="head">
    <action method="addJs">
```

```
    <script>http://s7.addthis.com/js/200/addthis_widget.js</script>
  </action>
</reference>
```

The AddThis button is now visible in our theme, allowing our store's customers to share our products with their friends and family!

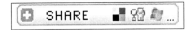

Summary

We have explored a few ideas on promoting and improving your Magento store with the use of social media, including:

- Using social bookmarks
- Using Twitter, the micro-blogging service
- Integrating customer feedback services like Get Satisfaction with Magento

There's still much we can do to improve our Magento theme, like creating print stylesheets. The best way to discover what works for your store and what doesn't is to experiment!

9
Magento Print Styles

So, your Magento theme looks good for those looking at it on their computer monitor. But what about those customers who'd like to print pages from your store? In this chapter, we'll look at:

- Examples of print stylesheets in other Magento themes
- Ideas on defining a good print stylesheet for your Magento store
- The creation of a print stylesheet for our Magento store, including what the layout files need to tell Magento

Viewing the print stylesheet

To view a web site's print stylesheet, you can select the **Print Preview** option from the **File** menu in most browsers.

The Developer Toolbar for Firefox (`https://addons.mozilla.org/en-US/firefox/addon/60`) allows you to select which stylesheet is applied by media type. Simply select the **print** option once the add-on is installed.

 Note that this does not quite present the print stylesheet as intended at times. For example, the `font-family` specified in the print stylesheet is sometimes ignored.

Print stylesheets in other Magento themes

A good place to start is by looking at what other Magento themes provide by way of print stylesheets.

The Default theme print style

The Default theme supplied with Magento, found at `http://demo.` `magentocommerce.com`, is seen by users when they first install Magento.

The store looks attractive for a computer screen, but it's not suitable for printing due to the following issues:

- There are large areas of dark colors, such as in the header, which will use unnecessary ink from your customers' printers.

- The three-column layout is unsuitable for printing.

- There is a lot of information that someone printing this page will not want—for example: **POPULAR TAGS**, poll, and cart features.

The print stylesheet provided by the Default theme styles the page's content to look like this:

The print styling for this theme is still not ideal for the following reasons:

- There is content in the footer of the page including the **Report All Bugs** link, which is unnecessary.

- The products as the primary focus of the page should be printed on the first page.

- The store's logo is not designed for a white background. Therefore, it looks ugly when a customer prints out a page from the store, which presents a poor image to those customers.

However, the print styling is more effective on individual product pages.

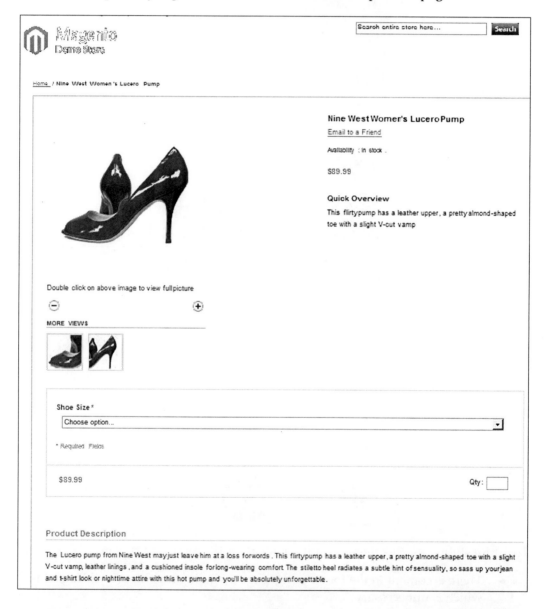

As you can see, the product photo and its details are now the primary focus. Although there is still some unnecessary information, such as product tags shown towards the footer of the page, it presents a much more printer-friendly view of the store.

Magento's Modern theme has similar problems with its print stylesheets, but a custom Magento theme can ensure that its print styling provides a better experience for customers.

Principles of good print stylesheet designs

We've seen that the print style for existing Magento themes is often not to the same standard as the styling for the computer screen and other mediums. Before starting our theme's print stylesheet, it's important to take note of some good practices in creating print stylesheets, as well as the limitations of print stylesheets.

Limitations of the print stylesheet

Many options that may be defined within the print stylesheet, such as whether or not to print images within the page, can be overwritten. This means that even with the best intentions when writing our store's print stylesheet, it will never be ideal for every browser and for every customer.

We just need to decide what information will be displayed when each page in our store is printed, and what information we wouldn't want to print.

Print preview

There is no reliable way to disable the print preview feature of a browser; quite rightly, as it should remain a choice of the web site's visitor.

Gecko-based browsers

One well-documented quirk of print stylesheets occurs in some Gecko-based browsers. When a long `div` element is floated with CSS, these browsers tend to ignore any content that is not printed on the first page where the `div` element occurs.

This can be quite easily bypassed with the addition of `float: none` to the relevant `div` tags in our store's print stylesheet.

What we should show

The primary content of each page should be printed. For most pages on our Magento store, this will include information such as the price and description of a product, as well as photographs of it.

Logos and store names

It's a good idea to include your store's logo and its name. If the printed page of your store is lost and found weeks, or even months later, then these will make it easier to recognize that page.

Promotional graphics and callouts

It's okay to print promotional graphics such as callouts, so long as they don't get in the way of the primary content of the page being printed. Generally, this means that it's better to make sure callout graphics are printed below or perhaps alongside the details of the product.

Bear in mind that some customers will print just the page that they want, which may mean that they don't see the promotional graphics when printed, and as mentioned, some visitors may even have disabled images from printing.

Links

A major problem with printing web pages is that the links within each page can lose their use. This is because, by default, the destination of the link is not shown. We can use CSS to append each link within the page being printed with the URL of the link, as we'll see later.

What we can hide

As we saw in the sample print stylesheets that we looked at earlier, there is also a lot that we can hide to lower the amount of content our store's customers need to print. This includes:

- Navigation and links to pages that are not related to the current page. There is little point in printing your store's navigation and footer links, as once printed, your customer won't be able to click on them!
- Search boxes—there's no use in printing this, as a printed copy of the page cannot be used to search.
- Popular product tags can't be clicked upon. Thus, they're of no use.
- Shopping basket—there is not much need for this to be printed most of the time, but this is a matter for you to consider.

Background images

Background images and unnecessary background colors can be removed using the print stylesheet with the aim of reducing the amount of unnecessary information that is printed.

Styling our theme for print

Generally, print stylesheets can be assigned in much the same way as screen stylesheets, with a `link` element being inserted within the head of the HTML document:

```
<link rel="stylesheet" type="text/css" media="print" href="print.css" />
```

Note that the `media` attribute is set to `print` to tell the browser that this style is to be applied for printing only.

Now that we have looked at print stylesheets in general, we can go about creating a print stylesheet for our new Magento theme. Currently, our Magento theme for the Cheesy Cheese Store looks like this:

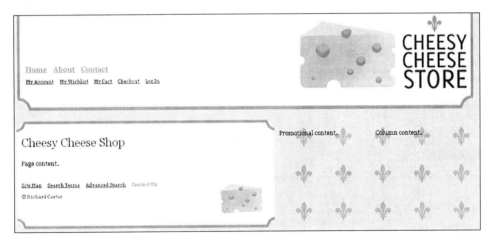

While we want the store's logo to be displayed, this theme is unsuitable for print for many of the reasons that we have discussed previously, those reasons include:

- There is a patterned background.
- There are many links that are not required to be printed in the navigation and elsewhere.
- The promotional graphics, shopping cart, and other features that are displayed in the columns are unnecessary.

Assigning a print stylesheet in Magento

In Magento, assigning the print stylesheet is a little more difficult, as we will need to edit the Magento layout files to ensure that the print stylesheet is assigned to each page. To do this, we need to edit the `page.xml` layout file in the `app/design/frontend/default/cheese2/layout` directory. Locate the line similar to that below the `default` handle in Magento:

```
<block type="page/html_head" name="head" as="head">
```

After this code in the layout file, we can insert a layout command to tell Magento to use our print stylesheet (if it is not already present):

```
<action method="addCss">
  <stylesheet>css/print.css</stylesheet>
  <params>media="print"</params>
</action>
```

Note that the print style is imported using Magento layout's `addCSS` method, and we specify that it is a print stylesheet within the `params` element. Next, we need to create a CSS file to be used as the print stylesheet. We can save this in the `skin/frontend/default/cheese2/css` directory of your Magento store's installation as `print.css`.

Styling Magento for print with CSS

We can style Magento for print with CSS almost as effectively as we can use CSS to style for the web. In particular, we'll need to pay attention to styling images, colors, and links within our store.

Images

There are three types of images that we'll concern ourselves with:

- The store's logo
- Product photos
- Other images, including background images set with CSS

As the store's logo is aliased to a white background, we can use it in our print stylesheet, and product photos will be fine too. The other images in our stylesheet will need to be hidden.

```
div.product-img-box img, #logo {
display: block;
float: none
}
```

Printing and colors

Most customers will probably want to print their page in black and white. To ensure that the background of the page is white, and that no background image will be printed, we can attribute the following CSS to the body element, and any elements likely to contain text such as headings and paragraphs:

```
body, ul, ol, dl, p, h1, h2, h3, h4, h5, h6 {
   background: #FFF !important;
   color: #000 !important;
}
a {
   color: #9C0;
   font-weight: bold;
   text-decoration: underline
}
```

This also gives any links that are still printed a blue color for color printers and a distinct gray color for monochrome printers. The "bolding" and underlining should reinforce the location of any links within the content. We can also provide basic styling for tables when printed:

```
th, td {color: #000 !important}
td {border-color: #AAA !important}
```

Printing and links

One obvious problem with printing our Magento store (or any web site) is that it will probably contain hyperlinks to other pages. When a page is printed, these links can be lost, but we can apply some CSS to print the destination of the link after the link's text, as follows:

```
#main a:link:after, #main a:visited:after {
   content: " [" attr(href) "] "
}
#main a[href^="/"]:after {
   content: " [http://www.example.com" attr(href) "] "
}
```

This CSS simply reads the href attribute from the link and adds it after the link in a div with the ID main using the :after pseudo-element of CSS. The second block of CSS, which uses the ^= attribute selector, affects links which have a href attribute, which begins with /.

Some older browsers like IE 6, do not recognize the `:after` pseudo-element or attribute selectors, meaning that the users of these browsers will not see the links' destinations after the link text itself. This is not ideal, but the previous solution at least provides some customers with this feature, without adding a great deal of complication to the process.

Printing and typography

While it's a good practice to use percentages or ems for screen stylesheets, for print, pts are more useful, especially because you can predict the size of the text as it will be displayed on paper more easily. At the same time, we'll change the font-family typefaces to be serif typefaces, which are easier to read on paper.

```
body {
  font-family: "georgia", "times", "times new roman", serif;
  font-size: 12pt
}
```

It's also a good idea to make any headings larger than the rest of the content to help retain the visual hierarchy of the page, as shown in the following snippet:

```
h1 {
  font-size: 24pt
}
h2 {
  font-size: 20pt
}
h3 {
  font-size: 18pt
}
h4, h5, h6 {
  font-size: 14pt;
  font-weight: bold;
  text-transform: uppercase
}
```

Printing and layout

It is best to avoid complex layouts or multi-columned layouts when creating a print stylesheet, as the width of the paper that the page is being printed on may not be able to accommodate multiple columns effectively. To combat this, we can use the following CSS in our print stylesheet:

```css
.header-top,
.middle-container
{
  display: block;
  float: none;
}
```

There are also areas that we can hide completely such as the navigation, search, shopping cart, and footer.

```css
.mini-search,
.header-nav,
.footer,
.quick-access,
.mini-product-tags,
.col-right,
.add-to-box,
.breadcrumbs,
.add-or,
.add-to-cart-box {
  display: none;
}
```

This CSS also hides the popular tag box, account links, breadcrumbs, and content in the righthand column, including the product comparison box.

Breadcrumbs

It is sometimes useful to leave the breadcrumbs visible, as it can give your store's visitors a reference as to how they found the page within your store.

This provides us with a stylesheet that's suitable for printing for our Magento theme, which looks like this:

Summary

Your Magento theme's print style is now ready for use. In this chapter we looked at:

- The principles of designing a good print style sheet for an e-commerce store
- Creating a print stylesheet
- Layout files, and how they relate to print styles in Magento

Finally, we'll look at deploying your Magento theme, and packaging it for the Magento community to enjoy.

10
Magento Theme Deployment

Magento is almost infinitely customizable, but there will come a time when you'll be happy to deploy your newly created Magento theme to your own store, or even release it to the Magento community. In this chapter, we'll look at:

- Cross-browser testing options for our new theme
- Deploying your theme on your own Magento store
- Packaging your Magento theme as an extension for others to use

Cross-browser testing

An important thing to consider before deploying your skin is how your theme displays in various browsers used on different operating systems such as Windows and Mac.

Testing your theme in every browser and on every platform might be too strenuous a task, as there are hundreds of combinations. Therefore, it might pay to consider the most likely browsers your store's customers will be using. For example, if your store is selling software aimed at Mac users, then it is more likely that your customers will be using Safari rather than Internet Explorer.

Popularity of browsers

There are a large number of browsers to choose from, but some are more popular than others.

HitsLink (`http://marketshare.hitslink.com`) reports that Microsoft's Internet Explorer has around 70% of browser users, while Firefox has around 20% of the browser market. Safari is reported to have a 6% share of the browser market, while Opera, Chrome, and Netscape have around 1% share each.

Wikipedia has a comparison of web browsers at
`http://en.wikipedia.org/wiki/Comparison_of_web_browsers`.

Browser-testing services

An alternative to testing our theme in only a select number of browsers is to use a
remote-access service or browser-compatibility testing tools, which allows you to
view your store's design as it would appear across a number of operating systems
and browser versions.

Browser-testing services only test the visual aspects of a theme (what
your theme looks like in a particular browser), and not the functionality
of your store. For example, there may be problems with older versions of
Internet Explorer or on some Internet Service Provider's connections. As
such, testing can only ever go so far.

BROWSERCAM

BROWSERCAM (`http://www.browsercam.com`) is a popular browser-testing service.

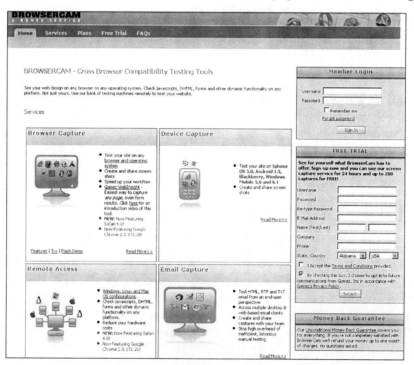

Although there is a monthly cost associated with using this service, you may be able to access a 24 hour free trial. Apart from showing you how your site will look on desktop browsers such as Internet Explorer, Firefox, Opera, and Safari, **BROWSERCAM** also allows you to see what your store looks like to those customers using handheld devices.

BrowserShots

BrowserShots (`http://www.browsershots.org`) has more limited functionality than **BROWSERCAM**, but it is free of charge.

BrowserShots

While it is more limited than BROWSERCAM, **BrowserShots** provides and huge range of browsers and operating systems as seen in the following figure:

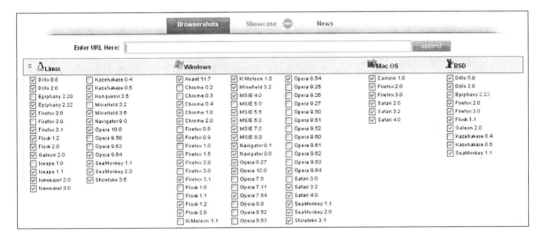

Deploying your Magento theme on your own store

Your Magento theme should already be ready on your store. However, before launching your store's new theme, there are a few things we need to do, such as:

- Make sure that the theme is set
- Turn template path hints off
- Turn the system cache on

Setting the theme

Your theme should already be set to display on your Magento store. However, if it isn't, then go to the **Configuration** option under **System** in your store's administration panel, as shown in the following screenshot:

From here, select the **Current Configuration Scope**, and make sure it is set to **Main Website as seen in the following screenshot:**

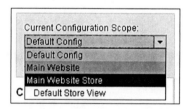

Under the **Design** tab to the left of the screen, you can now set the **Themes** setting to the name of your new Magento theme.

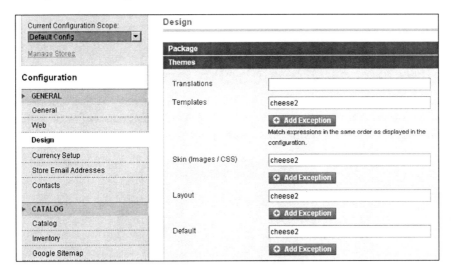

Once you've saved these settings, you should see your new Magento theme on your store.

Turning template path hints off

If you turned template path hints **On** while you were creating your Magento theme, then you'll need to turn these off before launching your store. You can do this from the **Configuration** panel located under **System** in your administration panel's navigation. From here, select the **Developer** tab under **Advanced**.

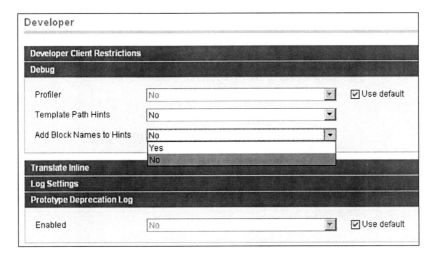

Make sure that you are viewing **Main Website** in the **Current Configuration Scope**, or else you won't be able to see the options above!

Turning the system cache on

Lastly, we can turn the system cache on. This helps to reduce the load on the server that your Magento store resides on. In your store's administration panel, select the **Cache Management** option under the **System** option in the navigation.

Once the **Cache Management** dashboard has loaded, select the **Enable** option next to **All Cache**, and click on the **Save cache settings** button.

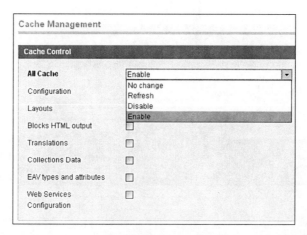

Packaging your Magento theme

If you want to make your Magento theme available for others in the Magento community, then you'll need to package it and make it accessible through Magento Connect.

Types of Magento contributions

There are three types of contribution that you can make to Magento, though only two will be of use to (most) Magento themes. They are:

- Magento Commercial Extensions
- Magento Community Extensions

The other type of contribution, known as a Magento Core Extension, is created by the Magento Core team. These are licensed under an **Open Software License (OSL)**.

Magento Commercial Extensions

Magento Commercial Extensions allow commercial entities to release themes for Magento under a license of their own choosing. There tend to be more restrictions on what you can or can't do with Commercial Extensions as compared to Community Extensions, so bear this in mind!

Magento Community Extensions

Releasing your theme as a Magento Community Extension allows others in the Magento community to use your theme as they wish. Themes released under this category can be licensed by any open source license.

As we're releasing our Magento theme to the Magento community, we can make use of the **Magento Community Extensions** option.

What to include in your packaged Magento theme

There are a few things that your packaged Magento theme will need to include, such as:

- The skin files, such as images, any theme-specific JavaScript, and related CSS files, in the `skin/frontend/default/cheese2` directory
- The PHTML template files for your theme, located in the `app/design/frontend/default/cheese2/template` directory
- Your theme's layout (XML) files in the `app/design/frontend/default/cheese2/layout` directory

You may also need to package your theme's locale files, if applicable.

Creating your package

You can create your package through the **Package Extensions** option, available under **Magento Connect** under **System** in your store's administration panel, as seen in the following screenshot:

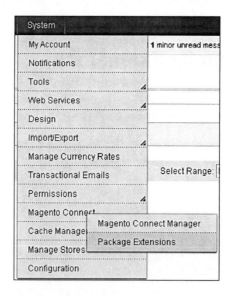

Package Info

You'll now be presented with the option to create a new extension and to give the package – your theme – a name, a summary, and a description.

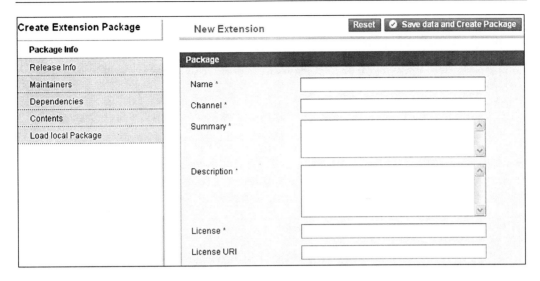

To start packaging our extension, we can fill in the fields required in the **Package Info** tab, as seen in the following screenshot

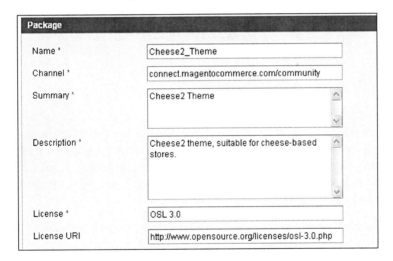

It's best to keep the **Name** of the extension clear of space characters — use underscores instead.

The **Channel** for our package is the Magento Community, as this is where we chose to release our theme. If you wish to release your theme for commercial use, then the value you need to use for the **Channel** value is `connect.magentocommerce.com/commercial`.

The **Summary** and **Description** of our extension should briefly explain what the theme is and what it is suitable for.

The **License** field allows you to specify what license your theme is available under. Some of your options include:

- Using an Open Source License — `http://www.opensource.org/licenses/`
- Using a Creative Commons License — `http://creativecommons.org`

As Magento itself is licensed under the OSL, the `cheese2` theme can also be released under this license. The next tab to the left, **Release Info**, allows us to specify the release information, as seen in the following screenshot:

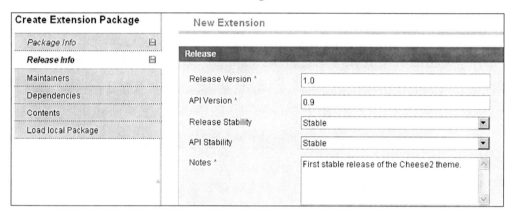

The release version is what you deem suitable for your theme. As we're releasing the `cheese2` theme as a first stable release, we can set the **Release Version** to **1.0**. Similarly, the **Release Stability** can be set to **Stable**, which indicates it is suitable for a "live" Magento store. If your theme is still in development, then select a relevant stability as this is helpful to Magento store owners looking to find a stable extension to use for their store.

Finally, use the **Notes** field to include any additional information about this particular release of the extension.

 The **API** and **API Stability** fields can be ignored, as they do not correspond to anything relevant with regards to themes in Magento.

Maintainers

The next step is to add **Maintainers** to the extension. This gives you the chance to specify those who worked on the theme. Firstly, you'll need to click **Add Maintainer as shown in the following screenshot:**

After selecting this, you're provided with the opportunity to fill in your **Name**, and your Magento Commerce login as shown in the following screenshot:

You can get a Magento username at
http://www.magentocommerce.com.

The **Lead** developer of the extension is required as a point of contact.

Dependencies

The next tab is for the **Dependencies** of our extension. As our extension is a theme, this doesn't concern us. However, we can safely put **5.2.0** as a value for **Minimum** under **PHP Version**, as this is the lowest version of PHP that Magento will run on. As our **Maximum** value, we'll use **6.0.0**.

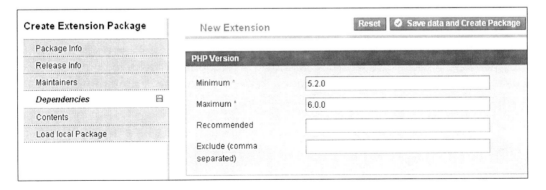

After selecting this, you're provided with the opportunity to fill in your **Name** and your Magento Commerce log in.

Contents

Next, we need to add the content associated with our extension under the **Contents** tab:

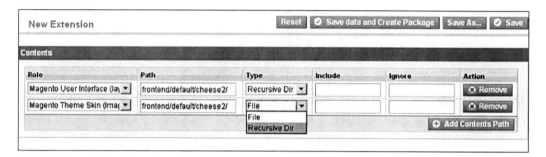

We need to create two contents for the theme. The first **Role** needs to be set to **Magento User Interface**, and the **Path** value needs to point to our layout and template files — frontend/default/cheese directory. The second **Role** needs to be for the theme's skin — **Magento Theme Skin** directory. The path needs to be the same as in the user interface — the frontend/default/cheese directory. Lastly, the **Type** values need to be set to **Recursive Dir** — this makes sure that every directory within the directories specified in the **Path field** are included.

We can now click on **Save data and Create Package**, after which our output extension will be accessible in the /var/pear directory of our Magento installation.

Sharing your theme with the Magento community

If you want to share your extension with other Magento store owners, then you'll need to provide the files exported here on the Magento web site (http://www.magentocommerce.com). Create an account (or log in to your existing account), and you'll find an option in the **My Account** section called **Magento Connect**, where there are two options:

- **Commercial extensions**
- **Community extensions**

Pick the relevant category for your new theme, and follow the instructions on the **Magento Connect** web site. You'll be asked to provide details for your theme, including a name and a description, as well as a screenshot.

Creation failed?

If the creation of your package failed, then make sure that the /var/pear directory has full read, write, and execute permissions.

Summary

Your Magento theme is now complete! In this chapter, we covered:

- The final tasks you need to perform before launching your theme on your own Magento store
- What your Magento theme should include
- Packaging your Magento theme for others to use
- A few licensing options for your theme

Index

Symbols

A

B

C

I

installing
  LazzyMonks module 127-129
  Magento's Blank Theme 38, 40

J

JavaScript files
  themes-specific, location 82

K

key
  for extension, retrieving 34-36, 127

L

layouts, Magento
  addCss action 121
  addJS action 121
  as attribute 122
  block, action attribute 120
  block, after attribute 121
  block, as attribute 121
  block, before attribute 121
  block, type attribute 121
  blocks 70, 120
  changing, on particular page 77
  content block 120
  customizing, XML used 72-74
  default handles 120
  default layout 119
  files 74
  handles 70, 74
  handles, using 120
  layout updates 119
  modifying 65
  modifying, CMS used 66, 67
  non-default handles 120
  reference element, using 121
  references 70
  removing 122
  structural block 120
  template path hints, enabling 68-70
  using, example 76, 77
  working 120

LazzyMonks module

installing 127-129

logo, Cheesy Cheese Store's Magento theme

callouts, removing 57, 58
changing 54-56
store's favicon, changing 56, 57

M

Magento
  about 5
  AddThis service used 135-137
  blocks 96
  cache, disabling 74
  CMS, accessing 43
  content block 29, 96
  customizing 8
  default layout 119
  default theme 7, 26- 29, 80, 140
  favicon, creating 110
  features 6
  hyperlinks, retaining 147
  interface 23
  layout, terminology 70
  layout files 27, 74
  layouts 65, 82, 119
  layout updates, using 119
  locales 24
  locales, downloading 81
  new theme, creating 94
  new theme, setting 110
  non-default themes 79
  page background color, setting 147
  shortcomings 6
  skins 82
  social media 125, 130, 132
  structural block 29, 96
  styling, for images 146
  styling, for print with CSS 146-149
  styling, links used 147
  styling, typography 148
  templates 30, 81, 82
  templates, skeleton templates 31
  theme 24
  theme, components 23
  theme, hierarchy 81

O

Open Software License. *See* OSL
OSL 157

P

package, creating
  API field 160
  API Stability field 160
  Channel 160
  content, adding 162
  content, Magento Theme Skin directory 162
  content, Magento User Interface 162
  dependencies tab 161, 162
  Description 160
  info 158-160
  License field, options 160
  Maintainers, adding 160, 161
  Notes field, using 160
  Package Extensions option 158
  Release Version, setting 160
  required fields, filling 159
  Save data and Create Package option 162
  summary 160
  theme, sharing with Magento community 162
pager.phtml file 102
print stylesheet
  assigning, in Magento 146
  background items, hiding 145
  callouts, displaying 144
  CSS, using 149
  default theme print style 141, 142
  hiding, items 144
  in other, Magento themes 139
  limitations 143
  links, displaying 144
  logo, displaying 144
  page content, styling 141
  primary content, displaying 144
  principles 143
  promotional graphics, displaying 144
  store name, displaying 144
  styling, on product pages 143
  theme, styling 145
  viewing 139

print stylesheet, limitations
  Gecko-based browsers 143
  print preview feature 143
product page, Magento theme tasks
  content hierarchy, improving 115, 116
  customizing 114, 115

R

Raspberry kids theme 9-12
Recycled Retriever theme 18-20

S

skeleton templates, creating
  assigning 96
  getChildHtml method 96
  layout structure 94
  saving 96
  viewing 95
social bookmarking, integrating with
    Magento
  about 132
  tools 132
  tools, AddThis 134
  tools, Socializer 133
Socializer 133
social media, Magento
  aspects, adding 125, 130, 132
structural block, Magento
  about 97
  content 97
  footer 97
  header 97
  left column 97
  right column 97

T

theme, Magento
  about 24
  Cacties 15, 17
  components 23, 25
  default theme 24-29
  examples 9, 12, 15-20
  features 21
  hierarchy 25, 81

[PACKT] PUBLISHING
Thank you for buying
Magento 1.3 Theme Design

Packt Open Source Project Royalties

When we sell a book written on an Open Source project, we pay a royalty directly to that project. Therefore by purchasing Magento 1.3 Theme Design, Packt will have given some of the money received to the Magento project.

In the long term, we see ourselves and you—customers and readers of our books—as part of the Open Source ecosystem, providing sustainable revenue for the projects we publish on. Our aim at Packt is to establish publishing royalties as an essential part of the service and support a business model that sustains Open Source.

If you're working with an Open Source project that you would like us to publish on, and subsequently pay royalties to, please get in touch with us.

Writing for Packt

We welcome all inquiries from people who are interested in authoring. Book proposals should be sent to author@packtpub.com. If your book idea is still at an early stage and you would like to discuss it first before writing a formal book proposal, contact us; one of our commissioning editors will get in touch with you.

We're not just looking for published authors; if you have strong technical skills but no writing experience, our experienced editors can help you develop a writing career, or simply get some additional reward for your expertise.

About Packt Publishing

Packt, pronounced 'packed', published its first book "Mastering phpMyAdmin for Effective MySQL Management" in April 2004 and subsequently continued to specialize in publishing highly focused books on specific technologies and solutions.

Our books and publications share the experiences of your fellow IT professionals in adapting and customizing today's systems, applications, and frameworks. Our solution-based books give you the knowledge and power to customize the software and technologies you're using to get the job done. Packt books are more specific and less general than the IT books you have seen in the past. Our unique business model allows us to bring you more focused information, giving you more of what you need to know, and less of what you don't.

Packt is a modern, yet unique publishing company, which focuses on producing quality, cutting-edge books for communities of developers, administrators, and newbies alike. For more information, please visit our website: www.PacktPub.com.

Magento: Beginner's Guide

ISBN: 978-1-847195-94-4   Paperback: 300 pages

Create a dynamic, fully featured, online store with the most powerful open source e-commerce software

1. Step-by-step guide to building your own online store

2. Focuses on the key features of Magento that you must know to get your store up and running

3. Customize the store's appearance to make it uniquely yours

4. Clearly illustrated with screenshots and a working example

Joomla! E-Commerce with VirtueMart

ISBN: 978-1-847196-74-3   Paperback: 476 pages

Build feature-rich online stores with Joomla! 1.0/1.5 and VirtueMart 1.1.x

1. Plone development fundamentals

2. Build your own e-commerce web site from scratch by adding features step-by-step to an example e-commerce web site

3. Configure the shop, build product catalogues, configure user registration settings for VirtueMart to take orders from around the world

4. Manage customers, orders, and a variety of currencies to provide the best customer service

Please check **www.PacktPub.com** for information on our titles

Drupal 6 Site Builder Solutions

ISBN: 978-1-847196-40-8 Paperback: 352 pages

Build powerful website features for your business and connect to your customers through blogs, product catalogs, newsletters, and maps

1. Implement the essential features of a business or non-profit website using Drupal

2. Integrate with other "web 2.0" sites such as Google Maps, Digg, Flickr, and YouTube to drive traffic, build a community, and increase your website's effectiveness

3. No website development knowledge required

4. Complete example of a real world site with clear explanation

Zend Framework 1.8
Web Application Development

ISBN: 978-1-847194-22-0 Paperback: 350 pages

Design, develop, and deploy feature-rich PHP web applications with this MVC framework

1. Create powerful web applications by leveraging the power of this Model-View-Controller-based framework

2. Learn by doing – create a "real-life" storefront application

3. Covers access control, performance optimization, and testing

4. Best practices, as well as debugging and designing discussion

Please check **www.PacktPub.com** for information on our titles

Lightning Source UK Ltd.
Milton Keynes UK
26 March 2010

151912UK00001B/61/P